Do You Want to Share That with the Class?

Do You Want to Share That with the Class?

Hilarious Anecdotes and Honest Advice for Primary ECTs

James Pearce

BLOOMSBURY EDUCATION

LONDON OXFORD NEW YORK NEW DELHI SYDNEY

BLOOMSBURY EDUCATION
Bloomsbury Publishing Plc
50 Bedford Square, London, WC1B 3DP, UK
29 Earlsfort Terrace, Dublin 2, Ireland

BLOOMSBURY, BLOOMSBURY EDUCATION and the Diana logo are
trademarks of Bloomsbury Publishing Plc

First published in Great Britain, 2023 by Bloomsbury Publishing Plc

This edition published in Great Britain, 2023 by Bloomsbury Publishing Plc

A catalogue record for this book is available from the British Library

ISBN: PB: 978-1-8019-9356-2; ePDF: 978-1-8019-9355-5;
ePub: 978-1-8019-9357-9

2 4 6 8 10 9 7 5 3 1

Cover illustration by Javier Joaquín

Typeset by Newgen KnowledgeWorks Pvt. Ltd., Chennai, India
Printed and bound in the UK by CPI Group (UK) Ltd., Croydon, CR0 4YY

To find out more about our authors and books visit www.bloomsbury.com
and sign up for our newsletters

Acknowledgements

This book has been a passion project that wouldn't have been possible without some incredible people. I dedicate this book to all of them.

To Charlotte, for your unfaltering love and encouragement over what can only be described as an early midlife crisis of writing a book.

To my family, for being as excited as I have been and always supporting me through life.

To those friends that have helped me with this process, for putting up with my constant questions and requests for feedback!

To all of my lecturers and friends at Kingston University, for three amazing years preparing me for the classroom and giving me the best start in my career.

To Stanners, a true friend and a rock during my career. I'm still so sad that you aren't here anymore, but you're never forgotten, especially when drinking a cuppa.

To Rachel, for being my mentor since I was a trainee teacher and mentoring me through a decade of my teaching career… so far.

To every pupil, colleague and parent that I have worked with during my teaching career, for your inspiration and for providing (without realising it) plenty of great material!

To my teachers, who helped make me the person I am today and inspired me to step into the classroom myself (especially Mrs Sellers, Mrs de Ferrer and Mrs Bailey).

To Joanna, Chloe and the team at Bloomsbury Education, as well as illustrator Javier Joaquín, for making my dream a reality and helping me get my ideas on to paper and into a book.

Contents

Contents

1 Introduction

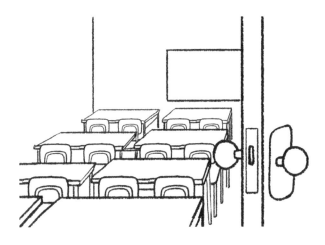

After a rushed morning filled with anxiety and stress, I had made it. In front of me stood the main door, and behind that was my very first school. My feet shifted as I took in the sight and waited for the moment to land; the uncomfortable feeling of new shoes rubbing against the backs of my ankles was already beginning to plague me. Despite that, for the first time that morning, a smile reached my face. I'd always had new shoes to celebrate a new year at school, but this time, they were adult size 13. I had just turned 22, and I wasn't a pupil any more. This time, I was the teacher.

As I stepped through the door that had started each day of my final training placement – as well as that fateful June day when I'd earned my first teaching job – the surroundings had never felt so unfamiliar. Yes, the beeps from the keypad sounded the same, the sign-in sheet was identical and the office area was already etched in my memory, but it just felt odd somehow. However, today was a new chapter, and that was never a bad thing.

My silent reflection was interrupted by a familiar voice.

'Morning! How are you feeling?' The deputy cheerfully smiled at me as she came out of her office.

'Hey! Everything OK?' my head of year asked as I saw him in the corridor. I answered with a semi-genuine smile and a committed nod, as I tried to hide my shaky hands and calm the feeling of nausea. I couldn't tell if the cause was nerves or my very real excitement. I just knew that I was keen to get going.

I reached my classroom a few minutes after 7.00 am, opened the door, switched on the light and walked (still plagued by the rubbing of the new shoes) across to my desk. Sitting down, I surveyed the scene like Mufasa and Simba looking at their kingdom from Pride Rock in The Lion King. Two thoughts sprung to mind as I took in the sight before me:

1. Everything that the light touched was mine – a new role, a new space to call my own and a new challenge to make the most of.
2. The room would never be this tidy, organised or quiet again!

I grinned a second time and took a deep breath as I turned on my computer.

'You've got this,' I reassured myself.

It has long been my ambition to write this book for two main reasons: 1) to share a realistic reflection of life on the front line in schools (including the funny highs and soul-searching lows) with those who are starting off in a primary classroom or are planning to join the ranks soon, and 2) to reminisce about how my decision to become a teacher got me to where I am today.

Some years have now passed since my first day, and despite trying to start writing this book a few times (on a family summer holiday in a mountain chalet, on the first night of a week-long residential and after leaving my other job as a weekend radio presenter), it was only after the COVID-19 lockdowns happened and I took some time to refocus my life that my passion project became my first priority. While the pandemic era was tough on teachers, I remain incredibly grateful that something positive has come from that time, and that it has meant that you get to read this book today.

Why a book for new teachers though? Well, truth be told, I have been passionate about supporting new teachers ever since becoming one. Since I left my alma mater, Kingston University, I've aimed to help those who've come after me, regardless of their training route, to be prepared for the profession that they have chosen to work in, and to work with Early Career Teachers (ECTs) as they face the reality of our job for the first time. My annual guest lecture to Kingston students is part serious pedagogical review and part stand-up act, which I am proud to deliver on their final day of university. I have also reached out and chatted to new teachers on social media and blogs, all to reassure people that we are a community and to provide them with the genuine ear and voice of someone living the teacher lifestyle along with them. All of that fed into this project and into the book that you are reading right now.

My hope is that this book will provide you with something that no other teacher's book or educational text does: a mixture of anecdotes, humour, research, facts, useful tips, honest experiences and thought-provoking questions to help you with whichever stage of the teaching journey you are on. Teaching isn't just an easy nine-to-three job where you get to play games all day (although there was a moment when I wondered why I was paying £3,500 a year for a degree in making maths treasure hunts and using puppets to explore a text). It is as tough as any other career path and just as rewarding. If you come away from reading this book feeling excited to get into the classroom and prepared to face the tough times, knowing that a good day will surely follow soon after, then I have done my bit.

When working out how to get the 195 days of an academic year into words, I thought that the best way was to focus on the moments that meant the most to me over my first year. Each chapter is about an experience or an event that you might come up against, and my own experiences of it. As a new teacher, I thought that no other teacher in the world must have gone through what I was going through, but I later found solace and satisfaction in discovering that those colleagues I looked up to and the lecturers I had learned from had all been through the same. I have added in some tips, tricks and general points that could help prepare you for what is to come and help you see the positive and fun side of what is truly an amazing job.

I hope you enjoy reading what happened to me from the minute I took my first Bambi-esque steps in the classroom to that movie-like moment when the car park barrier lifted and I drove off into the sunset for my first summer holiday, as 'School's Out' blasted from the car speakers. More than that, I hope it boosts your confidence to be the brilliant Early Career Teacher (ECT) that you are.

2 The night before

'3.15 am, quarter past three. In 12 hours, it'll be the end of the school day. There are only three hours left until my alarm is going to go off. I must remember to switch Jack's and Marium's seats round in the morning. Which door do I take my class through for assembly again?'

If it had been any other night of the school year, I would have taken some time to wonder why these six thoughts sped through my brain within the space of 30 seconds. As it was, I hadn't had a second of sleep since I turned out my light just after 10.00 pm. A well-intentioned early night had been the plan, but, five hours on, it seemed it was out of the window, just like the car alarm that had been keeping me company since the early hours.

My new colleagues had told me that every teacher finds it tough to sleep the night before a new year. Apparently, 'it doesn't matter if you're new or you've been teaching a long time; you'll feel a mix of nerves and excitement.' In all honesty, they were right. Of course, I was anxious about what was to come, but I was buzzing too. All my training came down to tomorrow. I couldn't imagine any other teachers were lying awake, thinking about seating plans and clock-watching as the minutes ticked by. They'd all be sleeping soundly, snoring contentedly, and would appear fresh-faced in the morning. My mind turned to how I could get rid of the bags that I'd be sporting under my eyes when I got to work in the morning.

I rolled over, put the pillow over my head and counted sheep. Desperate times called for desperate measures. Less than ten seconds had passed before my brain started turning my predicament into a maths problem. 'If a teacher is still awake at 3.19 am and has been in bed since 10.10 pm, how many more minutes of torment must they endure before they fall asleep?' I didn't have time to work it out, as the alarm woke me up. It turned out the answer was zero.

Sunday evenings are always the toughest part of the week, right? Your age and occupation don't matter; the anticipation (be it positive or negative) of that inevitable restart of the working week hits everyone hard. For teachers, when it comes to the night before a new term or a new academic year, the feeling seems to be multiplied by a thousand. Scientists haven't quite confirmed that number yet, but it must be in the right ballpark, because I have yet to meet a teacher who gets more than three hours of sleep during that night, or one who still has all ten fingernails intact after it. The 'night-before nerves' are a reality and the source of shared staffroom jokes on the first day of every term. Why we haven't had a sweepstake on which of us gets the least sleep I don't quite know!

While the phenomenon might seem negative, it isn't. It's a heady mix of anxiety, excitement, fear, anticipation and last-minute things to remember before the kids come in that keeps our brains alert and awake. It is a convenient way of managing the worries that we all have about starting or returning for a new school year. It helps us reassure ourselves that we have thought of everything – and if a new thought pops into any teacher's mind in the small hours, it can be a lifesaver. In fact, when I finally got to bed just before midnight for the start of this academic year, prepared and aware of what was to come, I made sure I had a notebook on standby, ready to write down any useful considerations that came to me in the middle of the night and to help move my mind back towards trying to sleep. If you do this, just don't be tempted to sit up for an hour and do a twentieth iteration of your seating plan!

One night, in those early hours, I thought I would search online for some advice and found that the NHS had published some ideas as part of their Better Health website (2023). I had to laugh over the irony as I scrolled through the suggestions of 'going to bed and getting up at fixed times… including weekends', 'avoid electronic devices at least an hour before bed' and 'do not force sleep'. Why? Because that's just not what us teachers do! The ideas were, of course, absolutely correct and I value what the medical professionals think, but I am regularly on my laptop just before bed (or scrolling through teaching memes) or forcing myself to get to sleep as it hits midnight. Plus, I am not giving up my weekend lie ins! If I wanted to drift off though, I had to listen.

Sleep, it turns out, is important for us teachers, and it is something that helps tip the scales towards a successful day.

If you do have a tough night like the inevitable 'September eve', then the best thing to remember is not to panic. You might spend the day yawning and sipping caffeine until you get the shakes, but it's usually easy enough to get through a day and reward yourself with an early night. However, if sleep continues to evade you then it is something to look at further. What is troubling you? Is it something in your mind or something in your sleeping environment? Are you finding it tough to switch off between work and home? Is there something you, your mentor or a colleague can do to minimise the issue that you are losing sleep over? It's important to ask these questions and really think about it because, as I've found out, being tired makes the job extremely tough.

An interesting *Guardian* article gives another perspective on it. The neurologist Judy Willis (2014) shared why sleep matters for teachers and what the effects are when we don't get a good trip to the 'Land of Nod'. She talks of 'woodpeckering' – the act of jerking one's head back upright after nodding forward for a snooze – which I have definitely succumbed to after a run of bad sleep. She also outlines the symptoms of not getting a good night's sleep: 'irritability, forgetfulness, lower tolerance of even minor annoyances, and less efficient organisation and planning.' To me, that's a list of things you don't want to be managing during a day with classes of children.

Rest assured, for most of us the second night of the school year is much better – except for a few times across the year, you'll be sleeping as soundly as your pupils in no time! In fact, the scary moment comes when you realise some of your pupils have a bedtime after yours.

Top tips and tricks

1. It sounds easy to say, but don't force yourself to sleep. Approach the night with the knowledge that thousands of teachers will be going through the same as you.

2. Schedule a sensible time to get into bed, in line with your usual routine. Trying to get to sleep too early can make things tougher. Alternatively, giving yourself a curfew can help encourage you to make the move and get into bed.

3. Try to pre-empt things that could keep your brain ticking over and manage them in the week before the return. Write out and work through those lists during your 'awake hours' instead of the precious ones when you should be sleeping.

4. Practise the usual healthy sleep strategies and techniques: a warm bath, candles, hot chocolate, a good book, relaxing music and some yoga in the evening can all help.

5. If you can't drop off to sleep, get rid of the clock and try lying down with your eyes shut. It sounds silly, and I thought it was just my parents' way of scoring an extra hour in bed when I was younger, but it does work. Even just resting your eyes and your body will help to revitalise you for a new day, and you might just surprise yourself when the alarm wakes you up after all.

3 Inset days

'Hey, everyone. I'm James…'

'Hi, James,' the group chorused back.

'… and no, I'm not an alcoholic… yet!'

Introducing myself to the staff at my new school was quite an intimidating moment and, me being me, I'd spent the first five minutes of the session wondering what I should say to cover the fact that I wanted the ground to swallow me up whole. It's funny how, as teachers, we don't mind standing up in front of 30 children, but when it comes to 30 adults, forget it. I'd gone with my usual humour tactic, which seemed to go down well. I was comforted by the smiles looking back at me as I sat down with my beetroot-red face. The paranoid version of me then took over, hoping I hadn't offended anyone in the process.

With my first impression in place, the In-Service Training (Inset) day could begin. It felt odd not seeing children traipsing up and down the corridors outside the hall, and even more odd to see adults sitting at tables like pupils. We'd be the ones learning today, so with the exceptions of coffee cups adorning the tables and most of us wearing jeans (a big advantage of Inset days at my school), the hall looked like a giant classroom, with our headteacher standing patiently by the board. He started off going through what we'd be covering, although he hadn't quite gone for the visual timetable offer. Our schedule looked busy and interesting for somebody new to the school: housekeeping, coffee break, safeguarding training, lunch, values (with another break – how spoilt were we?) and then an evaluation to finish the day.

As we dived into the housekeeping session, I got a good feeling inside. Things were starting to feel real now, and I was already beginning to feel like I belonged. It sounds silly and cliché, but even just seeing us all take out our diaries and planners made me realise I was in the big leagues now – no more of the plastic homework diaries I had as a pupil, or supermarket diaries I used as a uni student, for me. It's funny how the little things make us think (although I am never surprised by the effect that stationery has on a teacher). When the hour ended, not only did I know our whole-school targets and vision for the year, but my diary was filled with the dates of parents' evenings, class assemblies, Inset days, residential trips, non-school uniform days and tracking meetings. The rollercoaster of the year stretched out in front of me, and while I could see it was going to be a bumpy ride of highs and lows, I couldn't wait to leave the station and get going.

The rest of the day was much the same – discussion, tasks, Q&As, too much coffee and plenty of laughs with the others. When it came to filling in the evaluation form (which everyone rushes so they can get out the doors by 3.30 pm, because it's a rare novelty), I thanked the Senior Leadership Team (SLT) for making me feel prepared and part of the team. The Inset day really was the perfect way to start the ride of the first year, and luckily for me, the nickname 'Not-an-alcoholic James' didn't stick much past the first week.

An Inset day is a great way to ease into a new academic year, and most schools will use them as an opportunity to get all the members of staff together and start the year united. After all, as you will find out, consistency is key, and your SLT will likely do all they can to embed their fresh ideas for the three terms ahead within the staff team. I appreciated kicking things off in that way, because it reassured me that I'd be getting identical input and key messages to everyone else, so I wouldn't be trying to play catch-up or work out what was going on. One of my biggest anxieties coming into teaching was being out of my depth and making mistakes. If it's yours too, these sessions are a great way to remedy that fear early. They also give you a chance to settle in with all of your new colleagues and see the other faces you'll be spotting around the building in the weeks and months to come. Remember, you're part of that staff team now, and if you are all going to be on the same side, it's always beneficial to know who is there with you.

Officially, Inset days are specific days when staff training takes place and children should not be in school. We've seen them in schools since the late 1980s, when Kenneth Baker was the Education Secretary, and now they form part of the

School Teachers' Pay and Conditions Document. Yes, it's these extra days that add to our 190 teaching days and give us the directed 195 days that appear in most of our teacher contracts. The Inset days themselves will pop up across your school calendar, either by themselves or paired together, and their dates are usually decided before the academic year starts. This is because schools are very keen to let the parents know when they will be, and it is an advantage for us as teachers too as it means we can get the dates in the diary and know when those delightful 'four-ish-day weeks' are coming. My advice is to check your new school's website as soon as possible, because they might already be on there. Be warned though – some schools might not have five Inset days because they either aren't required to follow the same rules (e.g. private schools and academies) or instead have 'twilight training' sessions, where staff stay late for a couple of evenings and substitute those meetings for one of the quotas.

When it comes to the days themselves, they are usually quite a laid-back affair, despite their importance. Imagine being a teacher and getting to go into work without children and focus on developing yourself for a day – bliss! The school's senior leaders will have worked on an agenda, and each session will be focused on a key aspect of the curriculum or school that is important at that time. It could be anything: first-aid training, SEND-specific sessions, curriculum development, wellbeing for staff and students, creating a school development plan, EpiPen® and asthma training, safeguarding or even outdoor learning. You might have guest speakers or experts coming in or have training delivered by other colleagues. My first Inset day saw us spending an afternoon discussing and debating the qualities that we wanted to see in our pupils, before deciding on the six values that we would use to drive our school forward for the next decade – a pretty important and impactful decision!

Later on in this book, there is a chapter on why continuing professional development (CPD) is important for us as teachers, so I won't dwell too much on that now. But I will say that making the most of Inset days as a chance to learn and reflect is essential. You might find more experienced teachers rolling their eyes at another icebreaker activity or being told what to do for the 30th time in 30 years, but it is a worthwhile opportunity for you as a new teacher to get your head in the game, get on board with your new school and get learning.

Finally, an important point for those of you who will be starting in the classroom on a part-time basis: you may not be expected to attend every Inset day each year. In my experience, part-time members of staff might attend a number of sessions that reflects their proportion of the teaching week (so a teacher doing 40% or 0.4 of the week might be expected to do two days out of five, while a 60% or 0.6 teacher might be expected to do three days out of five). Alternatively, they might be expected to attend any Inset sessions that fall on their normal working days. Either way, this should be made clear to you with plenty of notice. If there are any doubts, ask your mentor or line manager for clarification. You might also be invited to attend sessions that aren't in your contracted allocation but would be useful for you; my advice would be to go if you can and ensure that you are offered some sort of time in lieu or compensatory pay, as stated in the School Teachers' Pay and Conditions Document.

Your attendance at Inset days and the reflections you take from them can be used as excellent evidence for fulfilling the Teachers' Standards.

Standard		Evidence
1	High expectations	The first Inset day year is arguably all about establishing the whole-school learning environment for the year and working together to decide on the expectations you will need to achieve this standard. Any training on creating the safe and stimulating space that children will be learning in and any decisions on how to inspire, motivate and challenge pupils will be relevant here.
8	Professional behaviours	Attending Inset days and working with your colleagues is a brilliant way to prove you are reaching this standard, because you're likely to be contributing to wider school life, developing your professional relationships and using it as an opportunity to improve your own practice. Notes, reflections or any certificates of completion should be sufficient evidence.
P2	Personal and professional conduct	Before the children even enter the building, you will be considering and practising the Part Two standards on the Inset day; forging those new colleague relationships and showing mutual respect will be key, as will building professional trust. You might even have specific training on safeguarding and other school policies, which are also important here.

Top tips and tricks

1. Use Inset days (especially those later in the year) as a chance to socialise outside of your normal circles. They are a brilliant chance to get to know your colleagues and find out more about those you don't work with directly. Everyone hates the moment when an icebreaker is announced or you're told to move tables to find someone you don't know well, but it really is a benefit for new teachers.

2. Take a note of key messages. Inset days are usually full of whole-school messages that you will need to know about. In my experience, you can expect to see school development plans, hear about whole-school targets, look through the school calendar and meet key figures from the school (including governors). All these bits of information are important for you and your practice.

3. Think 'food and drink'. Just because we tell children that they aren't allowed to eat and drink in class doesn't mean you shouldn't on an Inset day. Sometimes, sessions can be over two hours long, and you need something to keep you going. You should also check if lunch is or isn't provided, to ensure you don't end up going hungry.

4. Wear something comfy (if you are allowed). It's worth checking first, but I always go to Inset days in jeans and trainers. We learn better when we are comfortable (and we like to make the most of the opportunity).

5. Double-check at the end of the day. While most experienced teachers will rush off after an Inset day, take a few minutes to stop and reflect on what you've covered. Have you got any questions? Have you got any tasks to do for a future meeting? Have you got to add dates to your diary? Make sure you've got these in hand before you get going, or they will be easily forgotten.

4 The first day with a new class

The time had come. With three years of training under my belt, I felt surprisingly calm and ready. This was what I had wanted for years.

It was traditional at my school for all the staff to go out on to the playground as the gates opened on the first day, to be there to welcome the pupils in for a fresh, exciting year ahead. The playground was a cacophony of sounds that morning: chirpy children sharing stories of their summer, teachers trying to remember the names of the faces saying 'good morning' to them, and parents either keen to dash off and enjoy their returning freedom or emotional as they came to terms with the fact that their little ones weren't as little anymore. Set under a sunny September sky, the scene was perfect for starting off a new academic year.

After a while, the headteacher blew the whistle, and hundreds of staff and students spilled from the playground, filing towards their new classrooms. The hubbub grew as the children found their new lockers in the corridors and discovered just who they would be sitting next to in the first seating plan of the term (finalised at around 3.00 am). I found it all a bit overwhelming, but in a good way. We all had smiles from ear to ear, and the atmosphere was filled with positivity and anticipation.

After an age spent finding name labels on tables and managing to get the room quiet, we got to the register, and as the children answered with their 'six-word summer synopsis', I was proud to have remembered everyone's name from the induction day in the summer term. Taking the class list home over the summer was worth it!

With my teaching assistant (TA) taking the register back to the office, I sat on the unit at the front of the room and looked out over 30 faces peering back at me, waiting for whatever would be coming next. What I didn't expect was for this to be the moment that my mind went blank. All I had to offer my new class was a smile, covering up a vacant space where I'd thought my brain was. I'd planned for weeks with my year team for this moment. There was a timetable on the board to my left and piles of sheets ready for activities to my right, but my brain was having none of it. I went to speak, but just started laughing as the realisation dawned on me: I was now the teacher. A question then hit me: what on earth do I do now?!

The moment my mind went blank has been one of the memories from my first year of teaching that I've recalled and recounted the most because it was the first time in my career that the penny dropped and I realised it was all on me from that point on. Strangely, that thought didn't scare me. I was proud to be leading the learning in my own classroom and to have my name on the door (I still have the name plaque on my desk at home). It was just a surreal moment when my body and brain made the connection between all of the training and waiting I'd done for three years and the fact that the moment was playing out right now, in front of me. All I could do was smile and, despite the old teachers' saying 'don't smile until Christmas', I don't think I stopped smiling until the festive season!

The first proper day in the classroom is probably going to be the most planned day of the entire year; you have a whole summer to dwell on it and picture it. If you aren't sure what you should be doing, the first port of call is to ask your year team or your ECT mentor. Some schools will have shared activities across a year group (this obviously won't be the case for those in one-form-entry schools) and some will have school-wide tasks that need to be done. If you get to put your stamp on the day and come up with your own ideas, there are many different things you can do and thousands of online resources to inspire you. Think about what you want to achieve by the end of the first day: is it important to you that you learn everyone's names, plant the seedlings of your classroom culture, establish your expectations, build that all-important rapport or kick-start your behaviour-management strategies? Knowing what you want to prioritise and achieve will help you choose activities that will build those skills and get things going.

One thing I need to say is that while the first day is an important one, it shouldn't stress you out. I've read quite a few blogs and teacher websites over the years that say how vital the first day is for establishing yourself and your expectations, which it can be. However, it's one day of 190, and if you go home feeling a little bit disappointed or underwhelmed by the end of it, don't think for one second that that's your year written off. I've had some excellent first days and some that I wish I could have done again. Why? The children are different in each class, and while some come back to school with a prepared September mindset, some come back with a mindset partway through August. A common theme as we go through this book will be not beating yourself up if something doesn't quite work; there's always a tomorrow, and you should never dread that day. It's a chance to try again for the children as much as it is for you.

Oh, and for the record, the rest of my first day was a success. By 3.15 pm, every child had told me about their summer, filled in a one-page profile, written a letter to their future self (which was hidden in a 'time capsule' until the following July) and started their own self-portrait. More importantly to me, all the class had left with smiles on their faces and were happy to come back the next day for some learning, safe in the knowledge that they had a supportive teacher with their best interests at heart.

There could be some good evidence from your first day to kick-start your ECT paperwork and assessments:

Standard		Evidence
1	High expectations	As previously mentioned, this is the first chance you get to establish and embed your expectations with a new class. Creating new class rules together or doing an activity centred on how you and your pupils want the learning environment to be is a prime piece of evidence for this standard.
7	Managing behaviour	This is the first day to start embedding and implementing the school's behaviour policy to ensure that your classroom is a hotspot for great behaviour for learning. Any work you do on introducing or reviewing behaviour policies or strategies could be good evidence for this standard, along with any displays you've created in your classroom to link with it. It is usually a long process though, so don't expect to have them sitting silently on cue by the end of day one.
P2	Personal and professional conduct	The first part of Part Two is about treating pupils with dignity and building relationships that are rooted in mutual respect. There's no time like day one to start getting to know your pupils and constructing the rapport that will help in so many ways over the year. Just as with behaviour, though, don't expect everyone and everything to be perfect too quickly.

Top Tips and Tricks

1. Be prepared, but don't overprepare. You can't plan for every eventuality, so try not to put too much time into your first day. You have 189 more to plan and prepare for!

2. Be yourself. If it's the first time you are meeting the class or not, show them the teacher that you are. It can be tiring to try and be someone you aren't for a whole year. This doesn't stop you setting expectations though.

3. Learn as many names as you can. Knowing the children will be an enormous help over the year with assessment, behaviour management and so much more. On the first day, though, it's all about getting to know them and building that rapport.

4. Remember to be positive. I found it easy to be positive on my first day of teaching, but it isn't that way for everyone. However exhausting that first day is, celebrate the fact that your career is underway and you've started an amazing journey.

5. Remember, it's the first day of the year. It's a marathon, not a sprint.

5 Marking

I remember the moment when, aged six, I realised for the first time that I wanted to be a teacher. I was walking around the playground with my own Year 2 teacher explaining to her how fun it looked to listen to children reading and mark books with a special red pen. The moment I still recall most vividly from that exchange was the wry smile and laugh she gave in response. Fifteen years later, I realised why…

As quickly as the week to settle the class (and myself) into the swing of things had started, it was over. The real lessons had kicked in and, on my third afternoon, I sat down with a cup of tea and a new green pen (six-year-old me would be disappointed in the fact that I've only found one school that still marks in red). The first few books fell quickly as I cheerfully ticked the correct answers, dotted the incorrect ones, underlined the incorrect spellings and finished each piece with a meaningful comment and my soon-to-be-trademark smiley face. I was quite enjoying the experience and was genuinely proud of the work that we'd managed to do together that day. Maybe, just maybe, I could teach!

By the seventh book, I was into the swing of it, and the green pen was moving around effortlessly. By the fourteenth, I was halfway through my cup of tea and well on the way to getting these books down much more quickly than I'd anticipated. I knew some pieces of work would be boring to mark, but it really wasn't as bad as some teachers had made out. I was on my penultimate book when the door opened, and my mentor walked through to check in with me.

'All going OK with the marking?'

I nodded, showing him a piece that I was particularly proud of.

'Impressive. Looks like they picked it up quicker than mine did!' I was feeling quite chuffed at this point, until he came back with, 'Are you up to date with the marking policy? I can't see an LOA on these two books, and this one needs some circles around the missing full stops. In fact, that one you're doing needs those missing commas circled too.'

I stared at the pile of 'finished' books. I didn't mind making a mistake, because we all did that, but why hadn't I double-checked the policy before starting, and why was I realising this now that I was one book away from going home? Surely you can just tell where the children have earned a 'Learning Objective Achieved'?

Second cup of tea made, I sat down again and started from the top. 6.00 pm, here we come.

Marking is seen differently by every teacher: some see it as a necessary evil, some see it as an important tool and some see it as something that takes far too much time. Usually, the opinion is based on how long they have spent marking books that day, which day of the week it is and how many years the teacher has been teaching for. You might be lucky enough to find yourself at a 'no-marking school', which sounds like a dream to many of us in the world of education. However, the discussion about marking and assessment has been going on for years (and by years, I mean decades).

To give you a quick overview, marking and its use in schools have changed quite a bit while I have been in the classroom because of conversations between schools, unions, educationalists, the Department for Education (DfE) and Ofsted. My teacher from the days when I was six would often finish off a piece of work with a 'well done' and a sticker, having decorated my efforts with ticks and crosses. As lovely as it looked in the books, there was subsequently a shift, powered by Ofsted and the DfE, to ensuring that marking was more 'effective'. By this, they meant that marking should signpost what a child had done well and that any targets, corrections or extensions should be personalised to the pupil and piece of work. While this was a super idea, schools began to take it too far the other way. Elaborate marking policies were brought in, and comments stretched longer and longer. By the time I started teaching, a two-page 'big write' might have 30 or more marks on it, along with a short paragraph of comments. Unsurprisingly, the unions thought this was unfair on teachers and started to focus on reducing the expectations as part of the 'workload challenge' that they thrashed out with the government and Ofsted. Since then, marking has become part of the wider element of 'assessment and feedback' and is one tool that we can use to help assess pupil progress, to inform our teaching and to offer specific, impactful feedback to support our children's learning. The Education Endowment Foundation (EEF, 2021) says that 'done well, [meaningful feedback] supports pupil progress, building learning, addressing misunderstandings, and thereby closing the gap between where a pupil is and where the teacher wants them to be'. Oh, and as for Ofsted, they said in 2022 that they will not 'advocate a particular method of planning (including lesson planning), teaching or assessment' as part of its inspections or work, which again shows how the push is now towards marking that works for the children.

Plenty of work has gone into streamlining the way that teachers mark children's work, and your school's marking policy is your first port of call. Don't make the same mistake I did in that first week by trying to apply it from memory; print out a copy of the policy and have it by your desk. Most schools, in my experience, will have a handy one-pager in their policy with all the symbols you need. Use it as your go-to guide, and don't be afraid to check with your ECT mentor or colleagues if you have a question about how to use it. Consistency is key: you don't want to be using it incorrectly, causing your class to miss out on your input and support. While the aim of the policy is to reduce the time that teachers spend marking, be prepared for it to take time as a new teacher. During my first term, a class set of 'big writes' could take me up to three hours to mark, while my dreaded '150-book Wednesdays' saw me regularly leave work after 6.00 pm. Trust the fact that you will speed up as you familiarise yourself with the process and the policies; this was one of my biggest worries at the end of my first term, but now I power through my books at a much more rapid rate.

Marking is very much part of the Teachers' Standards.

Standard		Evidence
6	Assessment	Marking essentially has its own standard! Copies of your marking, comments or use of the school marking policy are all simple ways to prove that you are meeting this standard. It needs to be combined with wider tracking, monitoring and analysis, but some examples of day-to-day marking should feature as proof of this standard.
2	How pupils learn	Being accountable for your pupils' attainment, progress and outcomes is all part of what effective marking is about. By marking books using your school's policy and making use of feedback strategies, you are demonstrating that you are aware of the pupils' abilities and guiding them to reflect on their learning journey.

Top tips and tricks

1. Prioritise checking out your school's marking policy. This will be your guide to how your school wants you to mark the books and will be what you are held account to. Prioritise this as an early essential read, and ask your ECT mentor if you can't find a copy.

2. Look at your colleagues' books to see how they mark. I always found it useful to see the marking policy in action to help me understand what was expected of me. Make sure you always ask before you look, because some teachers don't take kindly to anyone else snooping in their books!

3. Remember that marking should be impactful. Marking isn't there to make the children's work look good; it is there to make a difference and to promote progress. If your school insists on comments being added to children's work, ensure they are signposting what is good or needs improvement.

4. Find a good pen. It's more important than you think! This is for every stationery lover out there (which, let's be honest, is every teacher). If you are sitting down to 150 books, you want to have a comfortable pen to use when marking. It's worth shopping around. Just make sure it's the correct colour for your policy.

5. Consider when verbal feedback might be more valuable. Sometimes it's easier to give verbal feedback instead of a long-winded comment that a child might not understand. If you have a marking policy with a code for 'verbal feedback', don't be shy about using it.

6 Questions

'OK, so that's a worksheet for Monday, the extension for Wednesday, number lines for Thursday and the lesson plans. Anything else? Nah, I think that's it…'

The weekend was imminent now – 5.00 pm on a Friday and one more job to do. The sofa was calling my name.

First things first, though: it was my turn to get the maths planning ready for my year group this week, and I was determined to get it right. I'd spent a few hours linking it all up to the National Curriculum and making flip charts with links and boxes that moved when you dragged them (an interactive whiteboard never gets old), with resources, differentiation and plenaries that I was quite proud of.

Now it was just a case of printing and copying everything, ready for Monday. I clicked 'Print' and selected the colour printer – a few extra pennies on the budget, but worth it for this first triumph, I thought.

I walked down the corridor towards the photocopier. The sensors were turning on the lights as I strode under them. 'Must be the last one left,' I thought. The school did have a ghost-town vibe about it. I turned the corner and stood patiently by the machine. I'd half expected my sheets to be there by now, but everyone knows that school IT has a habit of lagging behind when you least want it to (observation days, just before school trips, Fridays). Seconds turned to minutes before I came to the reluctant conclusion that my creations weren't coming. I was about to give up when I noticed the 'Enter PIN' box flashing on the screen. Two weeks in and I hadn't realised we even had printer PINs, let alone which code would crack this conundrum.

I rang one of my year-group colleagues to ask for help. The sound of chatting and clinking in the background told me they were already at the pub. Lucky! With a laugh, they gave me the all-important four digits for our year team and told me to get on with my weekend. It wasn't like I wasn't trying to…

Numbers pressed, code submitted, I looked at the mini screen as the wheel of doom spun slowly. Eventually it decided that I was worthy enough to have access, and I checked the print queue. Empty. Pfft! Technology! I tried going back to my classroom and sending it to the printer again. Nothing. Why hadn't I asked someone how to print before now? It couldn't be that difficult; I printed plenty of times in my other placement schools, and the printer at home didn't require me to be a genius. Defeated, I shuffled back and decided to call it a weekend.

Do You Want to Share That with the Class?

At least I'd managed another few hundred steps towards my 10,000 for the day.

Monday came around, and the printing and copier were top of my list. I got in early and popped in to see the same teacher I'd rung on Friday.

'Get everything done on Friday?' she asked.

I had no choice but to offer back a sheepish 'no', and decided I'd be brave and follow it up by asking her to show me how it was done. After a few clicks, just as I'd done on Friday, we went on the same adventure I'd been on a few days before. That is, until we turned right past the library and went through the Year 5 corridor and down to the colour printer, which I knew nothing about.

I couldn't hide my red face as we typed in the same PIN that she'd told me on Friday and saw four times as many print jobs as we were expecting. If only I'd thought about asking earlier!

If there's one thing I am always asking my children to do, it's to ask questions – if they are unsure, if they are curious or if they need help. It's funny how we don't always want to do that ourselves though, isn't it? In fact, most people I know will rarely put themselves forward to admit that they aren't sure.

This chapter is inspired by the guest lectures that I have done in the past for universities and how, when I went in to deliver my hour-long 'Welcome to the Front Line' lecture, I knew that what the trainee teachers really wanted was an hour to ask me every question they could think of. Oddly, I often find that when we switch from learning our craft to being in the teacher's position ourselves, we become more reluctant to ask and would rather dwell on a question or spend time trying to find an answer another way. I was the same when I started teaching; if I wasn't sure about something, asking someone for help was way down on my list of things to do to sort it out. It was like the old 'C3B4Me' classroom strategy, in which we'd encourage the children to look for the answer elsewhere three times before asking someone who would actually hold the key. Reflecting on this with some ECTs while I was writing this book, I realised I needed to write a chapter reassuring everyone that we shouldn't shy away from seeking help.

In the classroom, we ask our pupils questions to unlock their thinking and curiosity. Your mentor will likely do the same with you in your mentor meetings. We encourage children to ask questions so that we can assess their understanding and support their learning. While researching for this chapter, I found hundreds of blogs and articles that told me why it was powerful to allow my pupils to ask questions in class: encouraging creativity, motivating their thinking, enabling them to link their thoughts, providing the chance to challenge their ideas, developing their confidence and improving their cognitive abilities. So my question is: why do we, as adults and teachers, do this less often and think less of ourselves for doing it?

During your time as an ECT, I would advise and encourage you to push yourself to do the same as your pupils and ask for help or clarification. Please don't let a question become a burden and get in the way of you doing your best. Your mentor and colleagues won't look down on you or judge you for asking them where the paper cutter is or which resource you should be using for a lesson. In fact, most people working in schools will answer instinctively and won't even remember the question five seconds later.

This is another area in which your ECT mentor becomes a real shining light, because they are a perfect person to go to if you have something to ask. Their role in the induction process, as it says in the 2023 DfE guidance, is to 'work collaboratively with the ECT and other colleagues involved in the ECT's induction'. Working collaboratively means having an open and mutual working partnership where you feel confident and comfortable to ask questions and seek advice. If your mentor can't answer your question, they should know who is the right person to ask and help you do so. While your mentor might encourage more independence as you go through your induction years, they should always be there to help you and guide you.

Is there a bigger reason to be brave and ask? Well, yes. You being proactive in questioning is beneficial for your pupils too. As I gained confidence and experience over time, I'd often quiz our special educational needs and disabilities coordinator (SENDCo) about the needs of my pupils and ask her what I could be doing to be a more inclusive teacher, or I'd ask my headteacher to explain again exactly what I needed to do with my class for the whole-school project. Getting my facts in order enabled my class to get the best I had to offer, and it meant that they got the correct information first time. It let me have a greater impact on my pupils and their learning. My point is that there's nothing to be lost and everything to be gained by asking others to help when you are unsure. Being clear and certain helps you to be confident and correct as a teacher – and that's not a bad thing, surely?

Asking questions to your colleagues can even count towards your standards.

Standard		Evidence
3	Subject and curriculum	Teachers always need to refresh their subject and curriculum knowledge, so asking relevant questions to a subject or learning lead could demonstrate that you are developing your own understanding. Again, this can be evidenced through an email chain with questions being asked and answered.
5	Adaptive teaching	Meeting with your school's SENDCo or Inclusion Manager or your pupils' previous teachers can give you the chance to ask questions about the strengths and needs in your upcoming class. Any evidence of notes about specific approaches, support strategies or information about children from these meetings can be used as evidence.
8	Professional behaviours	Being proactive in asking questions to other members of staff in your school can help prove that you are being responsible for improving your teaching through advice and CPD. A printout of an email should be enough to evidence this.

Top tips and tricks

Instead of tips for this chapter, here are some questions to ask when you start at a new school.

- Are there coded doors around the school, and what are the codes that I need?
- How do I use the photocopier?
- If my computer isn't working, who do I call?

- Where are the staffroom and staff toilets?
- Am I able to use anything in the staffroom, or do people have their own mugs and tea/coffee?
- How can I reward a child for doing something brilliant?
- Who can I ask if I need support with challenging behaviour?
- Where can I go to top up my stationery supplies?
- What do I do if a child finishes their exercise book?
- Is there a presentation expectation for dates, titles, etc.?
- What time do things happen throughout the school day?
- Do I have a break duty? Where do I need to be based? Do I need a whistle?
- Where do I take the children at the end of the day?
- Are any children allowed to walk home by themselves?
- Do any children have certain people who are not allowed to pick them up for safeguarding reasons?
- Do I have to collect my class from the playground at break or lunchtime?
- Which assemblies am I expected to be in?
- Do I need to work with a small group during assemblies?
- Are there any weekly meetings I need to know about?

- Is there an expectation to wear casual clothes for teaching PE or Games lessons?
- Is there a staff dress code?
- What is the school policy on mobile phones in the school building?
- What are my new class like?
- Who is my ECT mentor, and when is our allocated time for meeting?
- Which staff members will I be working closely with?
- What is the expectation for meeting with my supporting adults to share planning or to debrief with them?

7 Staff meetings

There was a strange sense of relief as the final child left my classroom. Wet play, two children going home ill, a paperwork-heavy mentor meeting at lunchtime and a parent tour dropping in at the worst possible moment had all taken their toll. I was exhausted, but when home time came around, everything seemed manageable again. The only thing I had left was that night's meeting.

After the Inset days, online safeguarding training and a collaborative diary session, all of which my school referred to as the 'housekeeping meetings', it was time for a proper 'curriculum meeting' and the chance to develop the teaching and learning side of my practice. After spending three years at university, I wondered if there'd be a sense of familiarity to it; I was hoping I wouldn't be surrounded by people online shopping on their laptops or riding the waves of hangovers though. On tonight's menu was English, so at 3.25 pm I ambled down to the English lead's classroom with my diary and a cup of tea.

There was something quite funny about seeing teachers sitting at the children's tables and, if I was honest, acting like kids themselves. One of our strictest teachers was swinging on their chair, and a group of others were laughing about something obviously hilarious. Behind them, two of our Year 5 team were passing notes to each other, and adjacent was the head of Year 6, playing with a fiddle toy that they'd found on the floor. But the award had to go to one of the Year 3 team; instead of going for one of the digestives that had been kindly provided (as bribery, I am guessing) by our gracious host, they practically had a picnic on their table with grapes, crackers, a cereal bar and some chocolate. They put my cup of tea to shame. It was somewhat surreal, but taking in the scene made me realise that staff meetings may not be as scary or boring as I'd been warned in the past.

The meeting itself was much better than expected. We looked through some exemplars of children's work that demonstrated the expectations we were pushing for this year, watched some video resources that we could use in our classrooms, had an open and honest debate about what had worked (and not worked) last year and had a go at writing limericks (with some unsurprisingly rude results). I was even called on to talk about anything I'd picked up from uni the previous year that could be useful.

I admit that, beforehand, I was nervous about what these meetings would be like, and I wondered if they would be worth an hour of precious time when I had marking in my classroom needing to be done. It was worth it though, and it was a great opportunity to get to know more people in this new teacher team that I was a part of. By 4.30 pm, I came away with a couple of pages of notes, a sneaky third digestive and an appreciation of the fact that we had this time each week to invest in ourselves, for the good of our practice and the benefit of our classes. I just had to remember to bring more food the next week!

Dylan Wiliam, the educationalist who co-authored *Inside the Black Box* (a classic education text from 1998) and writes about assessment in our school systems, once said in a 2019 article for *TES* that 'every teacher needs to improve, not because they are not good enough, but because they can be even better.' It's important to realise and remember that these weekly meetings are your school's way of investing in you so that you can be even better for your class and for yourself. Throughout your teaching training, whichever pathway you've taken, you will have had lectures and sessions to teach you the ins and outs of the job. The CPD that you get now you're in school is all about topping up and refreshing that knowledge, as well as keeping you challenged as a teacher. We always consider how we stretch our more able pupils to keep them engaged and enriched, and that's what this does for us.

Now that I visit and work across different schools, it's interesting to see how different members of staff respond when they remember it's a staff-meeting day. Of course, we could all do with that extra hour or 90 minutes to get things done, but many teachers do appreciate a bit of time to come together as a team, have a good chat about the job and enjoy some snacks (because I know from experience that the better the snacks, the better the meeting!). The training and content of these meetings can differ week to week, and you will usually get a timetable in advance that tells you what is coming up. One week, you might be getting some input from a middle leader about their subject. Another week, you might have a guest speaker on an element of SEND. The following week, it might be someone representing a scheme you've bought into as a school doing some formal training. The best CPD programmes are varied and support your development across the curriculum.

As an example, one of the most surreal but most valuable staff meetings for me was when we had a gymnastics coach come in to teach us how to deliver our PE lessons. With no specialist knowledge whatsoever, I had been finding it tough getting the sessions from the paper plan and turning them into something worthwhile for my class. By the end of 90 minutes, however, I'd not only learned a lot about how to guide the learning better, but had demonstrated a forward roll with one beanbag between my chin and chest and another between my knees. I'll be honest: I was chuffed. I'd taken one for the team, and I felt I'd earned the applause the other teachers gave me when I successfully finished my move (although I am sure a few of them had hoped for a more humorous outcome).

The DfE has shown its strong feelings towards high-quality CPD by publishing standards for those who create and deliver professional development sessions for school staff. Its 'Standard for teachers' professional development' document (2016) says that teachers' training is 'a core part of securing effective teaching' and 'requires a pervasive culture of scholarship with a shared commitment for teachers to support one another to develop so that pupils benefit from the highest quality teaching'. An interesting report published in 2021 by the Education Policy Institute and the Wellcome Trust suggests that giving teachers 35 hours of high-quality CPD a year would give pupils a significant benefit over time. It is thought they could improve by two-thirds of a GCSE grade over their school lives, which could translate into better work opportunities and earnings as an adult. Both of these documents suggest to me that the drive for teachers to have opportunities to learn and grow won't be stopping any time soon and personally, I am very much all for it!

Oh, and one final quick note: when we talk about CPD, it isn't just staff meetings. While this chapter has homed in on those, you should also get the chance to go on courses relevant to your role in school, take part in online training and maybe even network with other staff members like yourself. I would hope that your school is making the most of the chances that are provided out there for you as a new teacher. If it isn't, be proactive in looking for courses aimed at ECTs or relevant to the areas in your practice highlighted as 'areas to improve' by your mentor or assessor.

Linking your CPD to the Teachers' Standards is straightforward.

Standard		Evidence
3	Subject and curriculum	This standard is essentially written about staff meetings! Your regular in-house CPD sessions will be excellent evidence for how you are developing your knowledge as a teacher. If you are lucky enough to have a guest speaker coming in, this will likely be even more valuable, and any notes you take should be a prime example of how you have met this standard. Push this further by reflecting on how it informs your teaching and learning.
4	Classroom practice	What you take away from your staff meetings should inform your practice, and therefore is likely to influence how you plan and teach. The fourth element of this standard requires you to reflect on approaches to teaching, which can be done through staff meetings where new schemes, strategies and approaches are explored. The fifth element of the standard could also be met through some of your sessions, especially if they're spent reviewing or developing the curriculum.
8	Professional behaviours	Attending staff meetings is a big tick for this standard: you'll be drawing on advice and support from colleagues, developing your effective professional relationships and improving your own teaching through appropriate sessions and courses. Any meeting notes or documents would be good evidence here, especially if supported by your own reflection.

Top tips and tricks

1. Take your diary or a notebook. Staff meetings often include messages, expectations or takeaway tasks that you will want to keep on top of. Not only will this help you stay abreast of what's happening, but meeting notes can also help with evidence for your Early Career Framework (ECF) paperwork.

2. Check what the meeting will be about and whether you need to take things with you. Sometimes you might need to bring children's work, examples of planning, resources or assessment sheets. It's a horrible feeling having to awkwardly run out of the meeting to pick these things up when you realise you've forgotten to bring them.

3. Be brave. Staff meetings are part of your CPD and an opportunity for you to grow as a practitioner. Make the most of the chance to ask and answer questions. Remember that you are valuable as you have fresh ideas, perspectives and (usually) the most up-to-date understanding of education.

4. Listen and learn. Use meetings to listen to other people as they share their experiences. It's a great way to learn more about your colleagues and develop your own knowledge.

5. Take a snack, but avoid a whole picnic! I remember seeing a colleague bring a full-on breakfast to a morning meeting once. It didn't go down too well.

8 Course days

The alarm went off.

Thursday morning. 6.00 am.

I opened my eyes and could see the usual early blur. The mornings were getting darker the deeper into the autumn term we got. I groaned as I reached over and eventually turned my alarm off. I've never been a morning person. Then it hit me – a feeling of genuine joy. I rolled back over with a smile on my face. because it wasn't a normal workday. It was a course day… and I didn't have to be anywhere until 9.30 am.

I heard my housemate's alarm go off. Being a teacher himself, he was confused as to why I wasn't even up and about as he was leaving for work. I was going to make the most of this late start, so after a shower – with more singing than the neighbours would have appreciated – a big breakfast and far too much glee as I pulled on a pair of comfy jeans, I was in the car and heading to a local racecourse. Sure, there was more traffic at this later time, but hey, I didn't care; I was belting out more tunes!

You must remember that I was 22 at this point. I'd never had a big job, never been to a conference and never networked in my life. That probably explains why I reacted the way I did when I turned up at the venue, parked my car and was met in the foyer with a fresh coffee and a pastry. Was this heaven? After signing in and getting my name badge, I explored more of this strange world: stalls selling teaching books and resources at discount prices, interactive games for the classroom being demonstrated and refreshments on tap. By 10.00 am, there were a few hundred of us in a room that was essentially set out as for a wedding (with added notepads and pens), and we were listening to our keynote speaker delivering his perspective on education. It was lovely to sit and listen to something uninterrupted and without the sound of children ringing in my ears. I scribbled in my notebook while sipping on my coffee and thought I could get used to this. Yes, the pastries and facilities were great, but it was beneficial beyond belief to listen to someone who had experience in education and still felt passionate about the children and the job. It felt promising to witness such enthusiasm and energy from someone who had been in schools for over 30 years. While they may not have been full time anymore, every word they were saying felt like it had come from time alongside us on the front line. Of course, the second-best moment of the morning was having a whole 30-minute break to go to the toilet without needing to rush, and to find another pastry and another hot drink to be enjoyed while it was still hot (although I was on the decaf by then).

By the end of the day, I left feeling revitalised and re-energised about my decision to teach. I felt like I'd stepped out of a 'teacher spa', with positive vibes, professional opinions and inspiring people being the order of the day. It was just what I needed to boost me and get my head back in the game. The children weren't going to know what had hit them when I returned on Friday with new strategies to focus them, a whole new room layout and three new approaches to teaching.

I want to start off with another honesty warning because, while this anecdote is very much the true experience of my first ever conference, I have come to learn that they aren't all as wonderful as that one. They can be a little dull at times, and the refreshments aren't always up to scratch (although I was lucky enough at one venue to have a three-course hot buffet and unlimited coffee and snack bar). However, that doesn't stop you from getting some much-needed inspiration and information.

As mentioned in the chapter about staff meetings, going out for courses and conferences isn't just a great opportunity to get some freebies and scoff yourself silly; it's a perfect time to pick up new ideas and tips from people outside your school community. If you are someone as nosy as me, you'll find yourself asking others how they do things at their schools and what schemes they use for this, that and the other. My advice from the off is to make the most of that chance to listen and learn. It's a unique chance to meet professionals with totally contrasting approaches and backgrounds to your own, and it can not only inform your own practice but influence your long-term teaching career. I know of two teachers who were so inspired by headteachers speaking at conferences that they ended up taking jobs at their schools.

Another thing to expect after a conference is to be asked to feed back to your colleagues. In the world of education, where 'value' and 'impact' are critical, your headteacher is more than likely to give you a chance to share what you learned and reflect alongside them what changes can be made. Now, this might sound terrifying, but it is a superb opportunity for you to play a key part in your school's development, and it's a demonstration of the fact that you are trusted as a professional to bring back your views and perspectives. It's a chance to be heard and to have a say.

If you are unsure how to approach a course day, chat with your mentor, because they will likely have been on plenty of them. In fact, they may have been on the same one you are attending! Ask what you should take, how best to make notes, what you should aim to bring back with you and how they think you should use it to reflect on your practice. The secret is trying to extract the most from it and using it to strengthen yourself as a teacher and practitioner.

There is one final point I want to make in this chapter. While it's a little off topic, it's mostly closely linked to the courses and conferences that you will hopefully get the chance to attend. If you find yourself in a situation where you aren't getting the invites, or your school says the funds won't allow you to go on as many CPD events as you'd like, there are two options:

1. Remind your employer that you are worth investing in and you are more than happy to be put forward for courses and conferences that would benefit the whole school. (This approach allowed one of my best friends to end up as his school's Outdoor Learning Leader after a few days' training out in some local forests!)

2. Use the wonderful resource that is the internet to find some talks and educators on social media, so you can keep refreshed and revitalised. I am always on the lookout for a good TED Talk video or podcast to listen to about teaching.

The bottom line is that now you're a teacher, you don't stop learning. Course days are a great day out of class (or 'day release', as I always call them), but they really can be much more valuable than that. You are more likely to get them as a new teacher, but they are something to always be on the lookout for and something you should push for throughout your teaching career.

Going to a conference won't just benefit your practice; it's brilliant evidence for your Teachers' Standards too.

Standard		Evidence
3	Subject and curriculum	Depending on the theme on your course, you will likely be evolving your subject and curriculum knowledge. Notes that you take on the day can be an easy way to evidence this standard, and will be even stronger when coupled with an example of the theme being referenced in lesson planning or self-reflection.
8	Professional behaviours	By taking part in course days, you will not only be out there representing your school, but will be listening, learning and reflecting on what to take back with you. Any notes and evidence that you've fed back to your colleagues or that you've adapted your practice as a result of CPD is strong evidence of this standard.

Standard		Evidence
P2	Personal and professional conduct	While the link is slightly looser here, I believe that course days can demonstrate that you are meeting Part Two of the Teachers' Standards too. By attending and engaging with the course, you are upholding public trust and maintaining high standards of ethics and behaviour, as well as developing your understanding of frameworks, policies and practices.

Top tips and tricks

1. Make notes. You might be able to feed back to your colleagues or to the SLT about what you have learned from the course. Notes help you to pass on those key messages, and they are super evidence for your ECF paperwork.

2. Network. Everyone is in the same boat on course days, and it's a good opportunity to get to learn more about other teachers and other schools. Ask questions, swap details and talk.

3. Take the chance to visit any exhibitors. If you are off to a conference, you might find a range of stalls with educational materials and resources at discount prices. I have bought a few brilliant educational books this way over the years and have even won some prizes from competitions too.

4. Reflect after the course day. After the fun and freedom, make sure you take the time to take stock of what you've learned and how you can use it to improve your practice. It's easy to move on quickly and not use the advice and wisdom, so ensure you are proactive with this.

5. Enjoy a restful day. Course days really can be like little holidays during a school term. Relish the late start (if you get one), crank up the radio in the car, drink too much coffee, appreciate having uninterrupted breaks and remember… there's no marking!

9 Guess who?

Did they have brown hair?

  Were they wearing glasses?

  What about a headscarf?

  Were they a woman?

  Were they a teacher?

  Until the last question, I could have been playing Guess Who? with my class during wet play, but instead I was standing in the office with one of my pupils, snot running from their nose, uncontrollable tears streaming down their cheeks and an ice pack working its 'magic' on his arm. The reason for my line of enquiry was to try and work out which adult from the playground had spoken to my latest patient during lunchtime.

Hiro had met me at the doorstep as the class trudged around for the afternoon lessons, one hand firmly gripping his injured arm and his eyes telling me that he was on the edge. It was the first time that a playground incident had made its way to the classroom door, and while I reminded myself of how to be an open and empathetic listener (another one of those uni sessions that stood me in good stead), I wasn't prepared for what was to come. The poor boy just couldn't get any words out between his bawling and the occasional breath that stopped him from passing out. Hiro couldn't answer questions with anything other than a nod or shake of the head, so once he nodded that he had spoken to a member of staff on the playground, my mission was to find out who it was and discover the secret behind what was going on. With the class silently reading and my TA stepping in to do the register, I took Hiro down to the office, for here was our version of Guess Who? – the staff board.

I remembered the pride of seeing my photo appearing on the board earlier that week with 'James Pearce – Year 4 Class Teacher' written below. I'd sent my parents a snap of it to show off the fact that I'd made it. The board was also a place of great wonder for the pupils; there was almost always a pair of children sitting on the comfy chairs in the foyer with ice packs or cardboard bowls, giggling as they saw what their teacher's first name was. But for now, the board was an essential piece of the puzzle, and the game was afoot.

Did they have brown hair?

Were they wearing glasses?

What about a headscarf?

Were they a woman?

Were they a teacher?

Hiro studied the board each time, nodding or shaking his head to answer my questions. Eventually, we narrowed it down to the final three, and I realised that I could have saved time by just asking him to point at who it was. Where was the fun in that though?

Mystery solved: it was Mrs Singh. The two of us trekked back out of the office in search of the lunchtime assistant in question. My only issue now was that I didn't have a clue who Mrs Singh was, but I hoped she could get me out of this conundrum. Maybe I need to spend some time swatting up myself!

One of the best things about working in a school is the fact that you become part of a community. It is different based on each setting (I've seen infant schools with ten staff members and primary schools with over a hundred), but for me, the people I've worked with really have become my greatest allies and the best support network I could have asked for. That's why I encourage every new teacher to start playing Guess Who? as soon as possible and get to know as many people as they can.

Arguably, some of your most valuable colleagues from the off will be your year team, your ECT mentor and your SLT. These are the people you will likely meet more than others, and they will play a part in your day-to-day work. Your ECT mentor will be very significant in your first two years, as you will meet with them regularly and they will be responsible for guiding you and your practice as a new teacher. While the relationship between mentor and mentee is professional, don't be afraid to share your work concerns and thoughts with them, because they can offer advice and support to help you overcome these.

Having a supportive and open year team is a real blessing, as they will always be your first port of call and will likely be there for reassurance. If you are in a one-form-entry school, you might get buddied up with another teacher as a way of ensuring you have that person to confide in but also get inspiration from.

There may also be times when you don't gel well with a team, or someone within your team. My advice would be to develop whatever working relationship you can with them and try to keep the communication channels open. I was once part of a major year-group disagreement that led to communications breaking down between the four of us as teachers. Our mutual aim was to make sure that we all kept talking, for the benefit of the pupils and to make sure the work didn't quadruple for us all.

As a teacher, it's important to also get to know those who don't work in the classrooms. There are so many roles and responsibilities in a school, and it can be confusing to know who leads what, and what each person does. I remember walking down a corridor in my second term and introducing myself to our lovely school cook, whom I hadn't met before. I assumed she was new, and I was going to welcome her, but she luckily let slip that she'd been working at the school for years. A lucky save for me!

I was fortunate to work with a wonderful office team, not just during my first year but in every school I've been in so far. They knew exactly what needed to be done, could tackle any problem and were always there for a quick laugh if you were dreading making a phone call to a parent. Whenever I work in a school nowadays, I always make a point of being friendly with the office staff when I sign in and thanking them whenever they help me. A bit of kindness goes a long way for these unsung heroes, and I would encourage everyone not to underestimate the 'guardians of the school gate'.

Your site team are also a good group to find and introduce yourself to when you start off in a school. It could be just one person or a brigade of caretakers, cleaners and constructors that keep the school site safe and sparkling. They often work hard to play their part and are very handy in helping to clean up unfortunate messes, fix broken furniture or sneak you a fan in the summer months.

There might also be the odd occasion when two worlds collide – for example, while we were doing our Islam unit in RE, my class loved having our caretaker come in to talk about why and how he was observing Ramadan. The children really appreciated being able to ask questions, and he left with an enormous smile on his face, his school community having shown respect and appreciation for his beliefs.

Ultimately, the adults you work with will keep you sane in the months and years to come. They will be there to support you, and you to support them. Teaching can be a lonely job if you shut yourself away, so be brave and be part of that team. Besides, it's true what they say: it's not what you know – it's who you know!

Working alongside your colleagues plays a big part in the Teachers' Standards too.

Standard		Evidence
1	High expectations	What better way to set high expectations for positive attitudes, values and behaviours than to be a role model? Demonstrate being friendly and polite with your colleagues to show your class how to act around their peers (maintaining professionalism, of course).
8	Professional behaviours	This standard is all about being part of the wider school community and developing effective professional relationships with colleagues. Keep copies of emails sent to your mentor when chatting about your meetings, to the office when planning school trips, to the site team when reporting a hazard – and any others that you think can prove this standard.

Standard		Evidence
P2	Personal and professional conduct	While Part Two focuses on children, it is important to be able to communicate with your colleagues for many of its elements, including reporting safeguarding concerns to a Designated Safeguarding Lead (DSL), demonstrating appropriate professional boundaries and modelling tolerance and mutual respect for others.

Top tips and tricks

1. Get to know people from right across your school community. The school can be much larger than your classroom, so challenge yourself to get to know a wide range of your colleagues.

2. Introduce yourself to key people across the school. From office staff to caretakers, from the SENDCo to the lunchtime team, everyone in your school has a part to play. I found that being proactive and saying hello to them first helped to start a positive and constructive rapport with them, which is a big advantage moving forward.

3. If you aren't sure what someone does, ask them (tactfully). There's nothing worse than smiling at someone for weeks on end, realising you haven't a clue who they are and then discovering it's your home–school link worker or school librarian. Ask

a colleague or your ECT mentor if you haven't been able to put a name to a face.

4. Know the chains of command and policies. There will be moments when you will need to refer parents or pupils to someone else within the school staffing structure, perhaps for a parent query or as part of your behaviour management. The key here is knowing who is the next in line and being confident in passing the issue on.

5. Remember, you can't keep everyone happy all the time. You might not click with some people from the off, but that's all right. It isn't essential to be great friends with everyone, but continue to communicate with them when necessary and maintain your professionalism.

10 The first observation

As I finished writing the date on the whiteboard, my hand wouldn't stop shaking. I couldn't tell if it was from being so nervous or from the third cup of coffee I'd had that morning. Unsurprisingly, I hadn't had much sleep the previous night, so caffeine had become my crutch. It was my own fault: I still hadn't got to sleep when 2.00 am came around, but instead of staying in bed, I had gone through the day's maths lesson and realised I just hadn't differentiated enough. I had ended up firing up the laptop and then I'd sat there thinking of a third way to support my less able pupils, and an extra challenge to push those who finished. Once the plans were tweaked, the resources were made and the flip chart was updated, it was 3.30 am. I had ventured back to bed, wondering what two hours of sleep could do to rejuvenate me.

After being in class for a month and easily having a hundred lessons under my belt (as well as three years of training), I knew I could teach. I knew my lessons were engaging and linked to the curriculum. I knew my class really well, and I was pretty confident that they could pull it out of the bag when I needed them to. For some reason, though, self-doubt kicked in like never before. It might have been the fact that it was my first observation with two people watching – my mentor and my assessor – or it might have been that I'd be teaching maths in front of two maths specialists. Whatever it was, I was frustrated with myself for letting the nerves creep in, while also being glad that they were there; after all, nerves prove you care about something, and they are brilliant at helping you bring your A-game.

What if the kids did let me down though? What if they misbehaved or were spotted fiddling under the tables? What if I'd pitched it all wrong or none of them got it? What if one of them decided to show off with a silly answer and use that day, of all days, to be a class clown? Argh! My head was full of too many 'what ifs' and not enough 'you cans'. As a very wise person once told me, 'what ifs' are useful for assessing risk, but 'you cans' are better at identifying what will actually happen and reminding you that you've got this.

By 10.00 am, I was a bundle of nerves, but my brave face was on. I'd reasoned with myself that if I couldn't teach then I'd be found out that morning and they would put me out of my misery. We could come up with a good enough excuse. No one would suspect. My thought process was interrupted by a knock at the door – two smiling faces, two clipboards and two blank forms on which my destiny would be recorded. (As you can probably tell at this point, getting dramatic is one of my typical reactions to stress.)

I invited my mentor and assessor in, showed them their seats and handed them a lesson plan (which I have always likened to going to see a play in a theatre and getting a programme).

'Remember to breathe,' my assessor said. I think she'd got used to my anxieties by now and could read my red face quite accurately. As I tried to hide the shakes in my voice, the curtain rose on the morning's performance.

'Who can remind me what we learned in yesterday's lesson?' Three hands went up, which hardly inspired me with confidence. 'Gwyn?'

'Umm, yesterday we looked at the first quadrant, which has all positive values. You gave us some coordinates and we had to use the x axis and y axis to plot them on the paper. Then we connected them up to create shapes. We had a bit of trouble with one of them, because we didn't know what the shape was, but you taught us it was a parallelogram.'

Honestly, I didn't know whether to cry happy tears, cheer or give Gwyn a high five right there and then. What a blinder! As it was, I went for a diplomatic smile and gave her a house point; the fist pump would have to wait until I could hide behind my cupboard door. We were off!

Even now, it makes me laugh to think back to when I was a trainee teacher and I thought that my final placement observation would be the last time I'd have to go through the nerves of being watched in the classroom. How wrong I was…

Some teachers (not just ECTs) find observations incredibly stressful, while others relish the challenge and the chance to show off their skills. The way in which you reacted to the idea of that second option will demonstrate to you which one you are! Either way, the place of observations in the ECF is not to catch new teachers out or find flaws to mark you down on; like the whole ECF induction process, the observations are there to monitor how you are doing, celebrate your progress as a teacher and find areas in which your mentor and your school can support and develop you, to help you become the best that you can be. I always used to get worried before an observation, and I still do, but I realise that it isn't there to trip me up, and I continually appreciate getting feedback that helps me improve. If it benefits the children I teach, I am all for it. The official DfE guidance document 'Induction for early career teachers (England)' (2023) says much the same: 'Induction should provide a foundation for ECTs and equip them with the tools to be an effective and successful teacher,' and the whole process should include 'development, support and professional dialogue.' Those words might not put to rest all the anxieties you have about your induction tutor coming in to see you in front of the class, but hopefully they'll remind you that it's part of the process and that it's intended to be useful.

The big question for this chapter is: how should you prepare for your observation to make sure that you're ready and you get the most out of it? The following is an outline of my thought process and the way I approach observations. If you are ever stuck on where to get started, I hope that this can provide some help.

First, think about the lesson you are going to teach. You might be asked to deliver a given subject, or you might get to choose. If you get to make the choice yourself, think about which subjects you feel strongest with, or which subjects you'd benefit from getting feedback on. Sometimes I've purposefully taught topics that I've felt were my weakest, as a way of getting advice and support. If you are given the subject or topic, you'll still have plenty of opportunities to put your stamp on the lesson with how you teach it. Either way, decide on your lesson early and give yourself plenty of time to prepare – no last-minute decisions the night before!

Next, think about your class. The best lesson observations are those that demonstrate a real understanding of the children they are aimed at. Consider what the children already know about the topic and what their next step is in the learning journey. How can you best support them with resources, differentiation and challenge? Are there any learners you need to personalise the learning for?

Then, use these ideas to plan your lesson. If you have pre-existing planning available to you, that can be a starting point, but it should be adapted for your class. Work out what your learning objective and success criteria will be. Devise tasks that will allow the children to prove that they have met their aims. Think carefully about what teaching input you need to deliver and what stimuli you can use to engage and motivate the pupils to learn. Also, think carefully about the pace of the lesson – make sure it keeps moving, but not too quickly.

Finally, always think about the practicalities of the lesson itself. How will you set up the classroom and your tables? Will you have resources out, ready to go, or will this just cause the children to fiddle and lose focus? Do you have adult support in the room that you need to deploy? Where will you put a chair for your observer so that they can see you teaching but also have a front-row seat for some excellent learning?

There are lots of elements to consider, but these are all things that you naturally think about and do on a daily basis; the secret to an observation is demonstrating that you *are* doing that and providing your tutor with the chance to see it. It's a bit like a driving test, in that you can be good at driving but passing the test is all about making it obvious that you are good at it – it's all a bit of a performance.

Most importantly though, when all is said and done, remember that it's a snapshot in time and that it's in the past as soon as it's finished. Celebrate your successes and keep your targets in mind. Teachers are notorious for dwelling on the downsides and forgetting to recognise everything that they have put into their work. Hold your head high and keep moving forward. You can do it!

This one might be obvious, but it's worth signposting how your observations feed into your evidence.

Standard		Evidence
4	Classroom practice	Feedback from your observation is arguably the best evidence you'll get when it comes to this standard. Ensure that you provide your tutor with a copy of your planning, which will enable them to provide you with comments on that too. Any written feedback will demonstrate your strengths and capabilities as well as your areas to improve.
8	Professional behaviours	The very nature of observations is to give you a chance to receive – and act upon – advice and feedback. This is part of taking responsibility for improving your teaching practice and professional development. Copies of feedback and reflective evidence on how you have used targets or further support to develop your teaching are valuable. Your observation is also a prime example of how you deploy support staff. A copy of a lesson plan should display evidence of this.

Top tips and tricks

1. Treat it like a showcase lesson and play to your strengths. As teachers, we tell children to show us what they are good at, and you should do just the same in an observation. It's a chance to prove to your assessor how fantastic you are, but it's also a chance to take stock of what you are best at and prove it to yourself.

2. Show that you know the class well. Aside from the planning and teaching of Teachers' Standard 4, your observer will be looking at how well you know the children. Use their names, display the respectful rapport you have with them and make use of your knowledge by adapting the lesson for their needs.

3. Make the 'headlines' clear. It might be part of your everyday practice anyway, but making your learning objective, success criteria and pupil progress obvious will help you demonstrate your worth.

4. Be prepared for questions and targets. When you are getting feedback after the observation, expect your observer to ask questions and give you targets for next time. The process is not there to catch you out or cause any doubt; it's a chance for you to share your thoughts and processes and professionally discuss approaches that might be easier or better.

5. Don't dwell, celebrate! When the observation is over, it's done. Focus on the positives and take forward the targets, instead of beating yourself up about anything that didn't quite go as you wanted (all teachers know that feeling!). Keep positive and reward yourself for all the effort you've put in.

11 Break duty

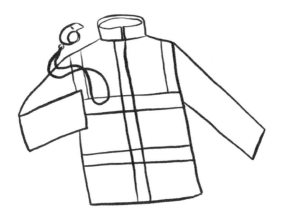

Clumps of soil flew from the crater that had been blasted into the muddy field. The offensive missile collided with the nose of one of those who had been brave (or foolish) enough to stand in the fray. Almost immediately, scarlet blood trickled forth, mixing with the brown streaks of mud that were smeared across his face. Loud noises shook my ears as I slowly made my way into the danger, armed only with a whistle and a fluorescent vest. Screams and shouts told the story of the unfolding drama. Two courageous beings each took an arm of the wounded and helped them over to me. The trio's brows were wet from rain and sweat. I knew exactly what I had to do.

'Michel, that's what you get if you try and get the football to bounce as high as you can and then stand directly over it. Come here. Let's have a look at you.' I gave him a tissue from my pocket and sent him off to the office. It was nothing a paper towel and a quick sit in the medical room couldn't fix. Emi and Sofia stayed by his side as they marched towards the building.

Shaking my head, I turned back around to look at the others standing in the Somme-like scene. 'None of you should be on the field anyway! Get back on to the playground.' The sea of sorry-looking and slightly traumatised faces made their way back to the safety of the playground, some more quickly than others. As the last one eventually made their way back to where they should have been, I laughed to myself for a moment. They never learn.

My moment's peace was stolen by the voice of a Year 3, who wanted to show me that she could do a handstand. My heart lurched as her feet left the floor and another inevitable injury approached.

It's quite easy to make break duty sound horrific, but it's honestly one of my favourite parts of the week. It's a chance to get outside for some fresh air and daylight (a luxury in the late autumn and early spring terms) and an opportunity to see your pupils in a new light. There's something very heart-warming about witnessing the most shy or diligent children letting loose, and observing friendships blossoming beyond what we see in our classrooms. As a teacher, it's valuable to see how the children behave and interact, because parents often ask about it during the first parents' evening. It is a lot easier to reassure them that their child is doing perfectly well when you've seen them playing with a group of others that week.

It was during my one of my regular stints on the playground that I realised how much children like to talk. I'm often ambushed by groups wanting to come and tell me their news and life story, even if I've never met them before in my life! I remember one girl spending a good five minutes telling me about her new puppy and how excited she was to be getting the dog that she'd always wanted. Funnily enough, it was that same dog that we bonded over when she joined my class three years later. She was impressed that I'd remembered Max for that long. While I would almost always rather have a conversation with those my own age, I'm always sucked in by the chats the children want to have with me, and I enjoy witnessing their happiness upon being listened to and valued.

Of course, it's well documented that play is also hugely important in children's development. The NI Direct website reminds us that 'play improves the cognitive, physical, social and emotional wellbeing of children and young people' and that it allows children to study and practice the skills of 'confidence, self-esteem, resilience, interaction, independence, curiosity and coping with challenging situations'. If what we teach inside the classroom will prepare them for work and surviving the big bad world, then the skills they pick up on the playground are what helps them to live their lives.

I must be honest (as I promised to from the start) and say that it isn't all roses; being on break duty does have its downsides. Firstly, there's the unfashionable high-visibility outfits that we're usually required to wear. There's no chance of hiding amongst a few hundred children with those on! Next, it means you miss out on a few vital minutes to prep your next lesson when letting the ringing in your ears subside, so you'll need to be ahead of yourself and get things ready before the school day starts. Additionally, it's a missed opportunity to pop to the toilet, which becomes a habitual routine for many of us. However, if you are lucky, or make a point of asking, you can usually find someone to watch your class for a couple of minutes while you get yourself a cuppa and do what you need to do before heading back in.

One final point: for those of you who (like me) wanted to be a teacher since you were running around on the playground as a kid yourself, being out on break duty is the time to live out another childhood dream: blowing the whistle. That feeling of power when one sound can make hundreds of children still and silent – incredible.

When it comes to Teachers' Standards and evidence, there are a few ways to weave in your break-duty experiences.

Standard		Evidence
1	High expectations	Taking on break duty is a good way of hitting this standard, as you will be playing your part in creating a safe environment for pupils while also interacting with them in a way that develops mutual respect and demonstrates positive values and behaviour. It is a great opportunity to prove your involvement in creating your whole-school culture too.
5	Adaptive teaching	While you won't be teaching during break times, you may have to be aware of the needs and strengths of the pupils you encounter. If there's a child who has a specific strategy to help manage their playground situations (such as Zones of Regulation), you can give evidence of how you adapt the way you interact with them, based on their needs. Likewise, you may have to be aware of social or safeguarding issues that alter your approach.

Standard		Evidence
7	Managing behaviour	Managing behaviour is a huge element of break duty and will be a key standard that you can evidence on the playground. You will be implementing rules and routines, applying school frameworks and communicating with a wide range of pupils, using a mixture of rapport and authority.

Top tips and tricks

1. Know your place and space. In many schools, those on duty have an area to patrol; make sure you know where yours is and stick to it.

2. Check if you have any responsibilities. Some teachers will be the first-aider on the playground or oversee a time-out area. Be clear on what you need to do.

3. Make sure you have your whistle with you. It can be a class teacher's job to blow the whistle and signal the end of break. It's something to check before an awkward search and a late return to the classroom!

4. Chat with the children. I love chatting to pupils 'on their own turf' and seeing their more social sides. It's refreshing to have an informal discussion with them, and it can help you to continue establishing your rapport with them.

5. Keep an eye out! Playgrounds are busy places, and many things can happen. Ensure that you are watching. If there is an incident and you aren't doing your duty, you could be asked to discuss it with the SLT at a later date.

12 School trips

The big day had arrived. Weeks of logistical planning (with the help of our awesome educational visits coordinator), drawing up group lists, writing risk assessments, finding parent helpers, collecting permission forms, redoing the group lists and generally stressing about flying solo on my first school trip were all over, and it was time to put the plans into action. It might sound a little overdramatic for just taking the class to a local museum on a coach, but – as I say to parents when they tell me it must be easy – many people would find it stressful with two of their own children. Just try it with 32.

After I'd taken a rushed register and asked 'Have you been to the toilet?' far too many times, we were ready to board the coach and get settled in. Memories of my pre-teaching days spent working in a theme park kicked in as I asked the pupils to raise their hands and show me that their seatbelts were fastened. I counted three times before finally giving the nod to the driver and taking my seat. The best bit of the whole day? I got to sit at the front! With great reward comes great responsibility though: I was in charge of the inhalers, EpiPens® and sick bucket.

A half hour later (after I'd banned the questions 'Are we there yet?' and 'When's lunch?'), we disembarked and walked crocodile-style to the museum. I swear that the children were walking as close to the kerb as humanly possible, just to test me, but a few reminders of how we'd all like to get to the museum in one piece did the job. The biggest test on the walk was getting across a road. It turns out that zebra crossings with a large group are really quite stressful, especially when you have half your class on one side, half on the other and you're standing in the middle of the road with a big fake smile, thanking drivers for their patience while telling the children to get a move on.

Once we made it to our destination, the time there couldn't have gone better: there was a greeting by the friendly museum staff (who told us exactly where the free tea and coffee was), some hilariously chaotic searches through the galleries to try and find a toilet and the obvious excitement as we all compared what we had in our packed lunches. Yes, I have to say that my class did very well, and it was after this first ever school trip that one of my classroom catchphrases was born: it truly was a 'proud teacher moment'. I was proud of them, but I was also proud of myself for managing to keep my calm and lead the trip. I even had some lovely conversations with the parent helpers, who told me that the group was full of praise for the 'new guy at school'.

When 3.00 pm came around, the trudge back to the coach was relatively plain sailing, albeit with Roman-style wax tablets and clay pots in tow. We'd even managed to make it to the gift shop, which meant most of the class were armed with something shiny or fluffy. With the children counted back on, seatbelts buckled and post-lunch sick bucket at the ready, we made our way back to school. The sense of relief was amazing, and while I still had the final handover to go, it felt so good to be nearly home and dry.

I will not hide the fact that I adore school trips. While I admit they can be hard work, some of my best teaching memories come from the days outside the classroom. Not only that, but I am a firm believer in our pupils getting the chance to learn beyond the four walls of the school building, because it is in the real world that they will use and apply the knowledge and skills that we teach them there.

Learning outside the classroom has been a popular way of supporting and securing education over the years, especially after the DfE (which was called the Department for Education and Skills at the time) published its own manifesto in 2006 encouraging teachers to elaborate and embellish their syllabus with trips to complement what pupils were learning. It stated that 'every young person should experience the world beyond the classroom as an essential part of learning and personal development, whatever their age, ability or circumstances'. The DfE's intention was to see an increase in meaningful educational experiences that linked to the National Curriculum and purposefully strengthened the learning that took place in the classroom. Two years later, in 2008, Ofsted published a report called 'Learning outside the classroom: How far should you go?' which said that schools were making the most of chances to take children out for trips but that, for many, the connection to the curriculum needed to be stronger. Yes, as exciting as it is to be out and about, it needs to be educational too.

Once you have worked out if a trip will be valuable and have impact on your pupils, the prep begins – and, as I mentioned, there can be a lot of it. Taking a class of children out of the safety of school requires a lot of thought, and this is something for ECTs to be mindful of. When I went on my first school trip, I did so as the only teacher, because the museum could only take one class per day for workshops. The list of things to sort out before we went was monumental and, while I had some expert help from our educational visits coordinator (who really was worth her weight in gold every time I planned one of these), I still had to think carefully about who would be in each group, where we'd sit on the coach, which parents we'd take with us, which medications I needed to have in my bag, who needed to sit near a bucket on the coach and how often I needed to count the children. Your ECT mentor and your colleagues will be founts of knowledge when it comes to this, so ask around to see if there's anything else you need to consider.

The most important document to complete before you go is a risk assessment. This is a list of things that can go wrong, what you will do to reduce them going wrong and what you will do if they do go wrong. It sounds terrifying, but it is actually a very useful document, especially if you haven't been on or led a trip before. I asked my mentor, our educational visits coordinator and the museum for help with my risk assessment as I was keen to get it right. Reading through it when it was completed, which every adult on the trip should do, I was reassured that I knew how to deal with some of the worst-case scenarios and prepared for those I might not have thought of.

Behaviour is essential to mention too, because children who find it tough to behave appropriately might struggle to manage when out and about. I always sit my class down before a trip and make it very clear what my expectations are when it comes to how they move around the place we are visiting and their noise levels. I remind them that we are a team and we should represent ourselves as the best that we can be. It is also a good idea to speak individually with children with SEND (and sometimes their parents) about the trip, to answer any questions that they have and show them what to expect. One of my pupils with autism spectrum disorder and anxiety enjoyed going on a trip to the British Museum because I'd printed him a map and he used it to guide his group around the galleries. It helped him understand where he was going and empowered him to be confident – a success I was and still am very proud of. This was something I used in my evidence folder to demonstrate Teachers' Standards 5 and 7.

Luckily for me, my first trip was local and was led by the education team at the museum as soon as we got in the front door, but some trips are teacher-led and take place further afield. On a week-long Year 6 residential to France, I had to lead my group around war memorials and a French city, all without speaking a word of the language. The points made by the DfE and Ofsted about trips being educationally valuable could be another thing to consider before going on your trip. Ask ahead to see if you will have a guide or any workshops and, if not, be prepared to create resources or fact sheets to help your pupils and the group leaders gain the most from the experience.

For me though, the important thing about school trips is making sure that they are fun and they will create a positive memory for your children to stick their learning to. I remember going to Greenwich as a pupil in 2000 for a whole-school trip celebrating the new millennium. We stood across the Greenwich

Mean Time line, and I learned about time zones. That memory still lives on the pinboard in my head, now adorned with sticky notes of the different time zones I've visited. Experiential learning really can be a powerful tool to promote overall learning and progress, so make the most of it and enjoy seeing your class in a whole new light.

School trips can be full of opportunities to gather some evidence for your ECF bank, especially with the amount of paperwork you can copy and include.

Standard		Evidence
2	How pupils learn	If you have made a clear connection between the National Curriculum and your trip, you can use this as evidence for Standard 2. The trip should be used as a tool to promote progress and support learning, and after the trip there should be a chance to reflect on what the children took from it.
4	Classroom practice	Planning for a trip is unlike any lesson plan you've done, but it comes down to the same fundamentals – you have an objective, knowledge and skills that you want children to acquire and practise. Any paperwork from the trip could demonstrate how you've planned for the learning – choose the best piece.
5	Adaptive teaching	Your risk-assessment document could identify the needs and strengths of your pupils and how you've catered for them in this unique learning environment. It might be that you have put those who need greater support with their learning in a smaller group with you to help them get more from the experience. Any of these decisions that are made clear on your plans or paperwork could be good evidence.

Top tips and tricks

1. 'Be prepared' is a good tip for many things in teaching, and this is definitely a time to be prepared! Grab a folder to put a class list, itinerary and list of emergency contacts in before you go, and ensure you have a copy of the risk assessment and medical list to hand too.

2. Ask colleagues for advice. It would be unusual for an ECT to go on their first school trip without a colleague, or to be the first to visit a new place, but it can happen. Whatever the arrangements, chat with colleagues, because they will have plenty of advice not only to help you manage the trip and the children's behaviour but also to help the class get the most from the experience.

3. Be clear on emergency procedures and policies. It sounds a little extreme, but this is important. Every school should have a procedure to be followed if there's an emergency on a school trip. Make sure you have a copy of it with you, and that you have any phone numbers you might need to call.

4. Stay calm. Everything will be all right, and although it can be tiring, you will enjoy the chance to be out and about with your class. Just remember to stay calm and confident, because this will help keep your class calm too.

5. Get to know any parent helpers. If you have parents coming along with you, have a chat with them. Not

only will this make it easier for you to work together for the day, but it's nice for the parents to see that their children's teacher is human and cares enough to build a rapport with them. Trust me, this can go a long way!

13 Assemblies

I couldn't believe it. After everything we'd joked about in the staffroom at lunchtime, they'd struck again, and now, of all moments.

It wasn't a tradition for new teachers to do assemblies at my first school, but somehow my name had made its way on to the rota, and the day had finally arrived. I'd been dreading it for weeks, because after watching the head, deputy and other experienced teachers delivering their valiant efforts, I couldn't fathom doing my own assembly while holding the attention of 400 children just before Monday home time. Don't get me wrong, we all loved making learning exciting and engaging (and I didn't mind playing the fool once in a while), but this wasn't a classroom we were talking about!

I thought back to my own assemblies at school – something calm playing on the speakers as we filed in quietly, a rousing rendition of 'Cauliflowers Fluffy' accompanied by a haphazard Mrs Jones on the piano and a meaningful story with its moral and meaning always coming a few pages too late to stop our stifled yawns. I was as guilty as anyone of a few hidden whispers and sneaky looks at friends, but I was now realising and worrying what 400 of them could look and sound like.

No. This was going to be different – an assembly that would be interesting and would wow the children into keeping their eyes forward and ears open. I could do that… I was pretty sure!

I trawled the web for ideas and thought carefully about the calendar. February. Valentine's Day, maybe? Pancake Day had already been taken (probably for the best, as I would have most likely fallen down the naive hole of getting children to flip pancakes at the front). It wasn't until I saw a trailer for the Winter Olympic Games one evening that it hit me: a perfect topic that would link to our school values and be full of interesting content.

The next few lunchtimes were spent on a daily search for inspiring videos, fascinating facts and a clear message for the pupils to leave the hall with. I wanted one of those 'wow' moments and to hear the kids buzzing about it when they left the hall – a very high bar to set for myself. I vetoed the idea of getting four children up to emulate the Jamaican bobsleigh team, as well as the kind offer from two girls in my class to perform their interpretation of Torvill and Dean's 'Bolero' (I didn't fancy seeing the ending of the performance on the hall floor – why is every school's hall floor so head-splittingly solid?). Eventually I'd whittled it down to showing the trailer of the upcoming Games, followed by looking at Eddie 'The Eagle' Edwards' journey of determination and resilience and a video montage of Winter Olympics best bits.

Eventually, the day itself arrived. After a final run-through at break time and a chat with my colleagues at lunchtime to get some strategies on how to keep the assembly going (with the usual hilarious unhelpful suggestions that belonged in the 'worst case scenario' box), I was ready. Well, as ready as you can be for your first assembly.

I smiled to the Year 6 helper at the front to cue her to turn down the music, and I took a deep breath. I felt like an Olympian standing at the start line myself. I could do this. I could keep the children focused and the behaviour up to scratch. My self-reassurance was almost beginning to work… and that was when it happened.

I managed three whole sentences before the laughter broke out and the whole school's attention was gone. I couldn't believe it. Just as my friends in the staffroom had predicted, the famous Phantom Farter had struck again.

While the first legislation around assemblies (as collective worship) came from the DfE in 1994, their value has never changed or diminished. In fact, while they might be nerve-wracking for some new teachers (and a prime environment for many humorous distractions), they are an essential part of the education that our pupils get from their time in school. It doesn't matter if those children are in Key Stage 1 or Key Stage 5, coming together to listen, share and engage is a valuable opportunity – and that's before we even dig into the content of the assembly itself.

Since the COVID-19 pandemic, it has really hit home to me how important it is to get the children in one place and give them that physical sense of community. As a year leader, a class teacher and a supply teacher, I've seen hundreds of assemblies, and I always take a moment to appreciate seeing all pupils getting the same key messages, celebrating their joint successes, engaging together with a topic or theme and having a shared experience that can lead to further chat on the playground or around the dinner table. In fact, I stumbled across a great TES article from 2021 by Sam Brown that brilliantly echoes those reasons and a few more, including the fact that assemblies give us a chance to set tone and expectation – a great way to ensure consistency across a school.

Often, assemblies are based on a topic or a theme. The growth of values-based approaches and schools has led to the rise of values assemblies: these typically focus on a trait, characteristic or value that the entire school community will be striving towards and focusing on during that period. The EEF stressed in its 2021 report 'Improving Social and Emotional Learning in Primary Schools' that it is important to develop social and emotional learning skills in pupils (especially those who are vulnerable or from disadvantaged backgrounds) and that whole-school approaches such as assemblies are a prime way to do this. Of course, in many schools, assemblies remain as a form of collective worship, so faith-related stories and songs are mainstays. These too feed into developing pupils' social and emotional understanding and give examples for children to consider and act on.

As the teacher at the front of the assembly, there are two main things to consider and prepare for: the planning and the behaviour management. When it comes to planning, a successful assembly is not one that's been planned ten minutes before or comes from a book you picked up on the way to the hall. Preparation is key and will help you feel confident in leading from the front. Some schools buy into schemes that link to their faith-based or values-based approach, or have general resources that are written specifically for a key stage or phase.

Check to see if your school wants you to use these first, because they can save you some time – although it is still up to you to work out *how* to deliver the assembly to make it engaging. If you need to come up with an assembly from scratch (like I did), have a think about topical dates, news items and stories that could inspire the school. There are plenty of assembly plans, stories, videos, slides and stimuli that you can find online. The usual teaching-resource websites are full of them too, and most are regularly updated with topical assemblies.

The main piece of advice I can give is to ensure your assembly is relevant and interesting to the children – and this is where behaviour management starts to creep in. Neil Hawkes (known as Dr Values, and the speaker at my very first Inset day) advises in an article he wrote in 2000, that 'it is vital that an assembly has an enriching quality. This can be accomplished by associating the theme of the assembly with the experience of the pupils. This makes the experience relevant and real to them.' I can say from experience that that is truer than I ever thought. If you want 400 children to listen and behave in a hall while you are doing an assembly, that's the secret. Keep it relevant, engaging and well paced, and give the children a chance to reflect on how your words relate to them.

The other key to behaviour in the hall, as with the classroom, is to be a role model of behaviour. Set that clear expectation from the beginning by waiting patiently at the front, standing quietly and smiling at those doing the same back. That's easier said than done; I chose to pace, triple-check my plan and do anything to avoid looking at the children while waiting for mine! It does work though, and it relaxes both you and the pupils as they wait for what you've got for them.

Finally, if the pressure gets too much or you feel like it isn't going as well as you'd hoped, remember that assemblies are short and that you are in charge. Take a second to breathe and keep going. You can get to the end of the assembly, and afterwards it becomes a learning experience. Nobody will be judging you either – the other staff in the hall will be grateful that it's you doing the assembly instead of them!

When it comes to your ECF framework and evidencing your practice, being part of or leading an assembly links to a few standards.

	Standard	Evidence
4	Classroom practice	Think of the assembly hall as merely a supersized classroom! Assemblies aren't a babysitting service but a carefully planned and delivered session that teaches, explores and shares something relevant with those in it. As any teacher will know, this doesn't just happen! Any evidence of your planning, your script, links to resources or photographs taken during the assembly could help you reflect and evidence how you stimulated pupil thinking, acted as a role model and encouraged pupils to articulate their ideas and feelings.
7	Managing behaviour	The odds are that you will make use of whole-school policies and strategies during your assembly which you will have seen, heard and practised before. Using them with children in other classes demonstrates your part in developing that positive and safe environment for all pupils in the school and establishing expectations. To take it even further, a great assembly will motivate pupils and give them the chance to reflect and articulate on what they have explored. You can evidence this by asking teachers to get their classes to write something down after the assembly and collecting them.

Standard		Evidence
8	Professional behaviours	You are contributing to the wider school culture and developing your feeling of shared responsibility for pupils across the school. If you are supporting colleagues in the assembly, the teamwork that happens before, during and after the event is another opportunity for you to practise and improve your professional behaviours. Furthermore, if parents are attending, there are chances to communicate with them and engage them in their own children's learning (see also Chapter 24, 'Class Assemblies'). This can all be evidenced using notes from your assembly plan and your own reflections.

Top tips and tricks

1. Check to see if a theme, value, stimulus or inspiration has already been set out for you before delving into the deep well that is online school assembly resources. Some schools have lists of books or videos pre-made for the term or year.

2. The internet is a great place to find assembly resources and full assemblies that people have created and shared. The important message here, as always, is to think before you use one. Is the message relevant for your school and your pupils?

3. Be reassured by adults helping you with behaviour management from the sidelines. Some teachers find it demoralising that their colleagues are

'undermining them' or 'sticking their oar in', but that couldn't be further from the truth. Behaviour management is a team game, and having your colleagues on hand to help allows you to continue leading from the front.

4. Watch other assemblies beforehand to get some ideas and a clear knowledge of how things work in your school hall. I had Planning, Preparation and Assessment (PPA) time during assemblies throughout my first year of teaching, so I took a few PPA sessions in assembly to see how it was being done.

5. Chat with your own class and use them to help you. Your class can inspire your theme, help if you need volunteers and give you feedback if you want to try something out on them before the assembly. More than that, they could make up a big chunk of the children in the hall, so if you can get them to act as 'behaviour ambassadors' you have one fewer chunk of the hall to worry about.

14 Parents' evenings

Parents' evening was one of those dates in my diary that I had been nervous about more than any other. There, I said it. Admission is the first step to recovery, after all. I didn't know if I was more worried about having to face up to the parents or how I would talk about my class for hours – I'd hardly been in the classroom for two months! I knew, deep down, that everything would be fine, but even the calmest of us have worries that we just can't shake off. This wasn't the time for a crisis of confidence though. I needed to get my head in the game. It was 3.20 pm, the last child had just been picked up from my classroom door and I was due at my desk in the hall in ten minutes. Just enough time to play one of my favourite games when in a spot of time pressure: Tea or Wee?

3.30 pm – Kiera

Well, that was the best way to start. Mum and Dad were waiting with a smile as I walked into the hall. They shook my hand and were pleased to hear Kiera had settled in well. She'd been a superstar in the class, so I knew it would be an easy appointment to begin with (which was why I wanted it there!). It turned out that Mum was my class rep too, and the parents' only questions were what type of wine I liked and which voucher I'd prefer at Christmas. They left on time and gifted me some biscuits to get me through the evening. I kept my fingers crossed that every appointment would be like that.

3.40 pm – Maurice

Spoke too soon. Maurice was a great kid, but he was a dynamo in the classroom, and he wasn't the easiest to manage when it came to social situations. I tried wording that positively, but between 'energetic and enthusiastic' and 'needs to work on listening to other people's perspectives and feelings', Mum's face changed. I think she knew I'd cottoned on. I hadn't been looking forward to that one, but it was my first tough customer out the way.

3.50 pm – Sophia

I'd been warned by one of the Year 6 teachers that some parents tended to forget we were teachers and not always parents. Sophia's mum seemed to be less interested in her daughter's work and how great she'd been doing with her maths; she wanted my thoughts on how best to manage her not getting on with her little brother and why I thought she was taking too long to get ready in the mornings. The irony was that she started the meeting by telling me I looked too young to teach or have kids.

Being 22 didn't feel young when I spent my days surrounded by eight-year-olds!

4.00 pm – Harry

With five children in the family, Harry's parents had practically booked in for the evening, so I wasn't surprised when I sat alone for the first five minutes, watching Harry's parents laughing with my colleague, who loved a chat. I'd been warned that he was always running late, and that if you have an appointment following his you'd just as well go and make a sneaky coffee. Next time, I decided, I'd advise Harry's parents to visit him last. I eventually managed to catch his eye, which served as a reminder to him that we should all be working in the same time zone. Harry's parents themselves were a joy, and I could see why their previous appointment had been such a laugh. Harry was a down-to-earth boy and gave everything a go in good spirit – a chip off the old block, it turned out. It was just a shame I could see my next parent standing behind them, foot tapping and arms folded.

4.10 pm – Pip

Zara's dad sat down with a notebook and made a point of telling me it was 4.14 pm. I could tell this was going to be a fun one. As he opened the notebook, it was clear that I wouldn't have to steer this meeting; he had already formulated questions, and all I had to do was answer them. Less parents' evening and more interview. The challenge was going to be making sure I answered consistently when his ex-wife came for her appointment the next evening.

4.20 pm – Suni

Suni joined the class a few weeks ago from Afghanistan. He didn't speak much English, but with the effort he put in and his cheeky smile, that boy was going to go far in life. I'd checked in with our SENDCo about his home life the previous week, and had realised that communication with Mum was going to be as tricky as it was when Suni first started. My solution was to write up a couple of paragraphs about how he'd settled in and how he was trying hard to pick up what he could, which I then translated online to make it easier for Mum to understand. After a warm exchange of smiles and our best attempts to swap pleasantries, I handed her my comments and was pleased to see a little tear welling up in her eye. We may not have shared much language or culture, but we shared that pride.

4.30 pm – Marie

Ironically, Marie's parents didn't really speak either, but for different reasons. I felt like a newsreader as I reeled off my headlines to two passive faces – no words, no nods, no smiles. Their daughter had done brilliantly so far that year, and I was smiling through every piece of news, but the deadpan duo didn't crack. Still, it meant I was done within five minutes and back on track.

4.40 pm – Peter

It was interesting to see the dynamics between different parents and how they revealed so much about the children. Peter's mum was scowling at her husband when he scrambled into the hall late, but was crying a minute later as I told them I'd put his artwork from this half term forward for a school prize. His targets of making sure he was ready for lessons on time and working on how he managed and communicated his emotions in class seemed very apt.

4.50 pm – Drew

A warning had come to me about Drew's parents: they were notoriously defensive and would question everything put to them. My approach? Charm and disarm. I going to make sure not only that I was in charge, but that I started my upcoming break on time. As I handed over Drew's latest test scores and shared how he was a great friend in our class community, they beamed with pride and stayed surprisingly quiet. If only I could have broached his presentation and handwriting with the same positivity.

5.00 pm

My one and only break of the evening. Two hours to go. 'Tea' lost out in this round…

This diary is a true reflection of my first parents' evening, from the nerves beforehand to the many types of parents and families who graced my desk in what felt like a weird version of speed dating. This was one of the milestones I had highlighted in my diary and one that I couldn't wait to both get to and get through. It turns out that my experiences are typical, because this is one of the most common topics I get questioned about by new teachers – but they always come back with positivity afterwards. No matter who they are, and whether they're parents themselves or not, teachers seem to be more anxious about the parents than the children when they start in the profession. I can reassure you that, while they aren't all as nice as Kiera's were, most parents are friendly and understanding and want the same as you do: the best for their child.

Ultimately, the benefits of communication between home and school are worth every smile, tear, awkward moment and tough question. The EEF believes (since its most recent research in 2021) that the impact of effective parental engagement (of which parents' evenings and home–school communication are integral parts) is moderately significant, advancing a pupil's performance by four months over their primary education.

Its evidence base cites nearly 100 sources examining how involving parents in their child's learning journey is strongly positive. Ofsted agrees, and said in 2011 that 'parental engagement can be a powerful lever for raising achievement in schools and there is much research to show the value of schools and parents working together to support pupils' learning'. From the perspective of a teacher, having parents working with you when it comes to a pupil's education is almost always essential to success and makes life a lot easier. Children spend most of their waking hours in the care of either you or one or more of their parents, so sharing achievements, goals and targets can only be advantageous.

Meeting your de facto teammates is a useful opportunity to see where each child is coming from: how much support they get at home, how much their parents prioritise their education and the structure and context of their family units all play a part. Remember though that whatever the story, parents will always fight for their children and will want what they think is best for them (even if we see it differently as experts in education).

Parents' evenings can be shoehorned into quite a few of the Teachers' Standards, but Standard 8 is one that I urge you to link it to.

Standard		Evidence
2	How pupils learn	These meetings are an opportunity not only to show that you are accountable for your pupils' attainment, progress and outcomes, but to get parents on board with encouraging their children to be responsible and conscientious when it comes to their own learning. Meeting notes exploring either of these two areas can be used as evidence.

Standard		Evidence
8	Professional behaviours	The final part of Teachers' Standard 8 says exactly what parents' evenings are all about: 'Communicate effectively with parents with regard to pupils' achievements and wellbeing'. Copies of any notes you've made about your pupils or records of meetings that you've had, along with any emails or documents from other colleagues (e.g. your SENDCo, year-team colleague or ECT mentor) to help ensure your meetings are impactful and accurate, will serve well as evidence.

Top tips and tricks

1. Preparation is key. As a new teacher, I found great reassurance in having notes on each child and data from our class tests with me during parents' evenings. Even if I didn't use them, having that information to hand meant that I could field most of the questions that the parents sent my way. It's also a good idea to note down any points you need to make and any potential trickiness or previous conversations you've had with those parents.

2. Start by asking for questions. This saves you from any last-minute questions that parents want answered before they leave. Not only does it give you time to work your way around to the answer

(especially if diplomacy is needed), but it means you have a better chance of staying on schedule.

3. Find some freebies. I always arm myself with worksheets, factsheets and one-page resources and have piles of them next to me when I do parents' evenings. If someone wants help with spelling, they get a copy of the year-group spelling list. Times tables? Wheels or grids. What's happening when? A class timetable. Support with homework? A copy of our homework guide. This is good for preventing a follow-up email after the meeting.

4. Keep to time. There is nothing worse than watching the clock as you get later and later, each parent more and more huffy that you've started late. Have a watch or timer on your desk so you (and the parents) can see the time, and don't be scared to move on when an appointment is over.

5. Ask for advice. As I've said, I was petrified about my first parents' evening, so I asked around for pointers from my ECT mentor, my year team, other teachers in the school and even the head. Get their thoughts and ideas. A chat with your class's previous teacher could also be useful, as they will have met the parents before.

15 Non-school uniform days

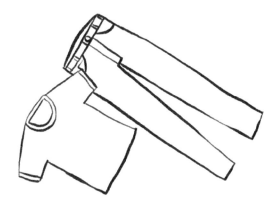

I'd been looking forward to this day for weeks, as had a lot of us in school. The children laughed at me when I told them I was excited; they said that teachers get to wear whatever they want, so I shouldn't be that keen to wear my usual jeans-and-T-shirt combo to work. It was an interesting point, but I wasn't going to let it dampen my spirit, because on this day I was going to be comfortable.

Just before I left my flat, my usual paranoia kicked in (so many of us have this anxious side, don't we?). Was it definitely non-school uniform day that day? I'd stick out like a sore thumb if I'd got it wrong. Plus, I'd surely get into trouble, because the staff handbook says no jeans for staff unless it's a school trip or a non-school uniform day. I resolved to check the school website again. But what if that was wrong too? Argh! Why did I do this to myself?

By 7.15 am, I was in the car and on the way to work. My jeans and T-shirt were on, and I was singing along to the radio. Life was good, and I'd managed to get over my earlier anxiety. No, I hadn't checked the website; I'd been confident enough to just go in… but I'd packed a whole work outfit in the back of my car, just in case.

Let me tell you, the relief I felt when I pulled into the car park at work and got a wave from my jeans-clad headteacher was immense.

Non-school uniform day is one of those little gifts that is surprisingly more of a boost during the school term than you realise, even if it starts somewhat precariously. I've always wondered if there exists a school that lets its staff wear non-school uniform every day, and thought how happy and effective those staff members must be! I remember 'non-uniform days' being great as a kid, and as a new teacher it is just as good, but for different reasons; while I was still settling into a new school and this new career path, any occasion when I could bring some of my home comforts into the classroom was a real help. It enabled me not only to feel more at home but to open up to my colleagues and community. I ended up having a big chat over lunch with another teacher about their Fleetwood Mac T-shirt, which played right into my musical tastes, and with a TA who appreciated the outfit choice that I'd gone for that day. She was quite surprised my T-shirt was a supermarket number!

Now, I haven't written a non-school uniform day chapter just to discuss my love of denim or my enthusiasm for getting the chance to 'dress down'; these days do have a couple of other important elements for new teachers to consider.

Behaviour can be trickier to manage on non-school uniform days, as the children's chance to ditch the uniform brings a lot of excitement and chatter. Be prepared for your lessons to be buzzier and to have to wait a little longer for the noise to subside when they all come into class. It's important to watch out for the social side of your class too, especially if someone seems to stick out because of their outfit. As an example, I had a stern word with a past class for not respecting a child's choice to wear their national dress into school when we had a 'wear yellow' day for the International Day of Happiness. Their kurta was a piece of art – yellow, silken and embroidered – but with many of my children seeing it as 'different', some made unkind comments about how Amir was wearing something that felt special to him but unusual to them. Honestly, it broke me, and I was so disappointed in those children – but it opened my eyes to a problem I hadn't pre-empted. The response? As a year team, we did some essential personal, social, health and economic education (PSHE) sessions around kindness, respect and the British values of respect and tolerance, as well as a whole new art unit on designing a kurta, learning from traditional designs, patterns and colours. It was safe to say that by the end of that year, Amir was proud to have worn his national dress that day and his family appreciated our apology and a photo of our year group's final designs.

Non-school uniform days are often linked to a charity, an initiative or a specific celebration. These occasions are brilliant for learning and can widen our pupils' horizons even more. If it is an awareness day, be proactive and engage with any whole-school activities that might be taking place during the day. I co-led a Children in Need assembly in my first year of teaching after a colleague invited me to get involved. We shared a montage of the previous year's hilarity and chose some appeal clips to watch, driving home the message to pupils that not every child was as fortunate as them… and I did all of this while dressed in my PJs and a dressing gown. It was a surreal moment, but I saw it as an opportunity to put myself out there and throw myself into a challenge.

Finally, it's also worth keeping an eye out for those children who come from families for whom times are hard or non-school uniform day isn't a priority. I once had a young boy who came in on non-school uniform day with his uniform on and was distraught to see that he had missed out. To make matters worse, one of his parents had passed away the month before, and the resulting chaos at home meant that I didn't want to encourage anyone rushing back with a change of clothes or adding to any guilt already being felt. Instead, I asked a TA to take him to our art cupboard and use anything he wanted in the fabric bags to decorate his uniform and 'punk it up'. It certainly won the approval of his classmates, and he was made up that he'd got to join in – but he could easily have missed out if we hadn't been mindful.

Unsurprisingly, non-school uniform days aren't easy to use as evidence against your Teachers' Standards, but they could be shoehorned into Teachers' Standard 8, especially if you participate in or lead an activity that contributes to the wider school ethos (such as an assembly, a whole-school activity or a visit linked to the cause you are raising money for).

Top tips and tricks

1. Check the rules. Make sure you are allowed to wear what you want on non-school uniform day, because there might still be guidance to follow as part of the staff handbook (e.g. some schools don't allow ripped jeans, even on non-uniform days).

2. Bring something in. Get involved and help the cause by mirroring whatever the children need to bring. I always brought in a pound coin for the charity we were supporting or a bottle for the bottle tombola at the upcoming fair.

3. Make sure you have the right date. As I said earlier, I am paranoid about getting things like this wrong. Check the date to avoid turning up in non-school uniform on the wrong day.

4. Look ahead. When checking the date, have a look at what else you've got coming up that day; you might not feel right wearing jeans and a sparkly top to that key meeting you've got after school.

5. Be yourself. Allow this to be an opportunity to develop your rapport with your children and show your school community who you are. This is a great chance to wear your style and personality on your sleeve (or as your sleeve!) – but keep it appropriate.

16 Performances

There's something strangely satisfying about watching your class or your year group performing on the stage. It doesn't matter if it's for a leavers' assembly, a music concert or a show to celebrate one of the many religious festivals, it's heart-warming and humbling to see them giving it their all as their adoring audience watches on. Well, most of them anyway.

My first performance of the academic year was the Christmas carol concert, which involved three weeks of blood, sweat and tears for us teachers as we painstakingly practised every song, every entrance and the classic sitting-down and standing-up routines. I told them countless times to face the front and stop talking, and if I'd had a pound for every occasion a child just walked off the stage mid-song to ask to go to the toilet, I'd have been able to fund our festive production going on a worldwide tour! Yes, they could be in Reception or in Year 6 and the experience would still be filled with moments that make you want to pull your hair out – but it's all in aid of that 'aww' moment when it's showtime. Luckily, for that first performance I had my year team with me to bring some humour, which certainly kept us going.

One of our favourite activities (aside from the sweepstake on which pupil would ask for a bathroom break first) was to spot the usual suspects when it comes to child performances…

The unenthusiastic

This child always seems to be front and centre of the stage, delivering their words and singing the songs with a total lack of enthusiasm or energy. They are usually the sole reason for their teachers waving a huge 'smile' sign at the back of the hall, prompting no reaction from them while their classmates pull their cheek muscles.

The overdramatic

Every lyric and line is delivered with perfect annunciation and usually comes with improvised gestures and facial expressions to match. This child's ability to throw their voice to reach the back rows is admirable, and they easily steal the show. Always remember their name, because you could get yourself some free theatre tickets one day…

The faller

Less 'Defying Gravity' and more letting gravity take its course. I don't think I've made it through a year without seeing a child take an accidental stage dive. In rehearsals it's quite easily spotted, but when this child falls mid-show, you only know it's happened from the parents' gasps.

The misheard lyric singer

Since the dawn of time, children have been making up alternative lyrics to the songs they sing at school to annoy their teachers, but this is the child who just never grasped the words in the first place. I will never forget watching as a Year 6 pupil sang confidently along to the classic leavers' song 'Goodbye My Friend' with the line 'Goodbye, my friend, this is the bend'. Who knows what he thought he was singing about?

The wrong-direction dancer

I love this one – they never fail to make me smile. As much as we practise our left and right, there's always someone who just can't get in sync with the others. I always tell this child that if they can't stay in time, they should just enjoy it and give it their all. Why should they lose out on the fun?

The wannabe director

Too frequently I have found myself negotiating with this child, who has not only choreographed their own routine to a musical number, but now wants to share it with the rest of the year group. They don't quite understand that 120 children doing forward rolls on an already cramped stage is a health-and-safety nightmare and won't make it past the risk assessment.

The one who's found their calling

Usually, this is the child for whom every school day is a long slog. They give it their all in class, but most likely don't quite manage to hit the learning objective. Put them on a stage, however, and suddenly they are smashing it with their performance. It turns out they will be all right in life after all.

The one who brings a tear to your eye

I have never made it through weeks of rehearsals without there being a moment when I've cried – not from any stress, but from those moments that catch you off guard. For me, it's usually during the big show, when the child who's been wobbling with their words and confidence during the practices just knocks it out of the park. That, or the moment we managed to get 120 children to respectfully bow their heads and turn off their electric candles after singing 'Pipes of Peace' – absolute magic.

The phantom farter

My old assembly nemesis usually pops up at least once every time we get the kids onstage. You can usually narrow it down to the child by watching the ripple effect of disgusted faces spreading around them.

Back to my first carol concert – after weeks of practice and re-practice, the time came for the big night. We hadn't managed to run through it all once without a break or some sort of drama. Although the parents find it endearing when things go awry, we wanted the kids to nail it and show themselves how brilliant they can be. More than that, we didn't want to lose face with the other year teams. We didn't need to worry though, because our pupils brought the house down. There wasn't a dry eye in the room by the end and, to this day, it is one of my favourite teacher memories.

Performances are lovely moments in the school calendar and a true reminder that it is important we develop the whole child as they journey through their school lives, not just the academic elements. For some pupils, this will be their time to shine, and it's always the one who has been quiet all year who suddenly shows a side that none of you knew existed. It might sound cheesy, but it's true.

Due to the range of education settings and the fabulously multicultural nature of society nowadays, school performances can happen at any time and for any reason throughout the year. Gone are the days of primary schools just having an annual nativity, with a gold star made out of cardboard and plenty of cotton-wool balls affixed on to a flock of children from Reception. No, the season's calendar has grown somewhat, and I've been lucky enough to see leavers' shows, spring singalongs, Diwali dances and firework-night concerts. Whatever the occasion, the experience of learning a new skill, song or routine, practising it and performing it in front of an audience is incredibly valuable for children, and it is a process that many of them will encounter in later education and adult life. It isn't just actors, actresses and musicians that need to be able to perform; spokespeople, politicians, lawyers, entrepreneurs, tour guides, salespeople, coaches, poets, authors and so many more jobs require people to be able to learn something and recite it to others or make use of public speaking. As teachers, we practically do this daily, when we perform our latest lesson plan to a usually willing audience of pupils. In a world where we are responsible for preparing our pupils to forge a career in an industry that may not exist yet or live a life in a society whose characteristics we can't predict, what better than to use opportunities like a performance to let them develop their confidence, flair, resilience and memory? They could just be the skills they need to succeed.

Getting involved in your school performances is not only fun, but can link with the Teachers' Standards.

Standard		Evidence
1	High expectations	It's important to create an environment where children feel safe and confident enough to have a go at performing and know that they are contributing to the team effort. Setting high expectations and combining these with the values of teamwork and trust are all part of what this standard is about.
7	Managing behaviour	Behaviour can be tougher to manage onstage than in the familiar confines of a classroom, especially if you have many more pupils involved. Try out new techniques and observe your colleagues when they are trying to regain control of the room, because their methods can feed into your own practice.
8	Professional behaviours	Performances are another opportunity to be part of your school community and contribute to the ethos. Any evidence of you taking the lead or playing a part in running school performances can be evidence for Teachers' Standard 8.

Top tips and tricks

1. Get involved. There's nothing more boring than sitting on the sidelines during rehearsals and performances. If you have a knack or talent for the performing arts, let your team know and play your part.

2. Observe your pupils. Take note of those who shine in this environment and those who surprise you onstage. It makes for great parents' evening and report comments!

3. Enjoy the experience. Even if you have time pressure bearing down on you, rehearsals and performances bring some light-hearted fun to the year and are moments to make the most of.

4. Collaborate (and laugh) with your colleagues. I would say that the weeks leading up to my first school performance was a real bonding time for me and my year team. We laughed and cried together over those weeks, and it was a chance for me to feel part of the group.

5. Push yourself. Primary teachers are often known as 'jacks of all trades, masters of none' – but even if drama, dance and music really aren't your thing, try taking yourself out of your comfort zone. There will be children onstage who are petrified of performing, so seeing a teacher giving it a go might provide them with an inspiring role model.

17 Staff nights out

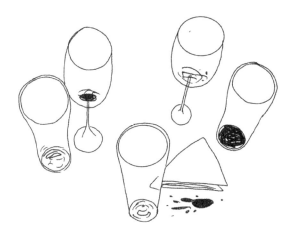

The only sound coming from the staffroom was the occasional groan, followed by a hiss as I jokingly threatened to turn on the light. Three teachers had crash-landed on the comfy chairs, covering their eyes and heads with their coats. I joined them, admitting defeat. Whoever had planned the staff night out to be the evening before the final Inset day of term could only be described by a word that I don't want to use in this book.

Our number grew as the clock ticked towards 9.00 am, many of us nursing a headache and a suspiciously dry mouth. Maybe there was a bug going around? Our hopes of that were dashed when one of the teachers who hadn't made it to last night's shindig arrived looking shiny and smug. The headteacher came in to rouse us minutes before our first session, 'The Art of Differentiation', promising us some bacon butties at break if we could pull ourselves into the hall. I felt like once again I was a teenager being dragged up and out after a heavy night with college friends, or a uni student cursing their alarm after a student night. At least I could count my lucky stars that our music training had been and gone during a different Inset day; nothing would have convinced me to get involved with any recorders or glockenspiels in my current state.

To his credit, our headteacher came good on his promise, and by 11.00 am we'd trudged back to the confines of the darkened staffroom armed with bacon sandwiches and cups of strong coffee. It was there that another university flashback came to haunt me: the post-match debrief.

'Is it just me, or did I see someone going up to a man and asking to stroke his beard?' Laughter erupted for a second, before the groans returned as the pain hit our heads.

'No, I remember that. Can't remember if it was before or after we tried doing headstands up against the bar though.'

'That explains the massive bruise on my leg! Trying to explain that to my husband this morning was an interesting conversation.' More laughter was stopped short by the pain.

'OK, OK, this is what I want to know: did any of the rest of you see the parent in the room?' It was gasps, not laughs, this time, as worried faces dared to peek out from under the hands hiding them.

'I wouldn't worry too much. He won't say anything. He was on a date… and not with his wife.' Forget the hangover; this just got interesting!

Every time I give a guest lecture at a university or do a talk for new teachers, I mention how I thought the nights out when I was a student were messy… until I became a teacher! It seems that spending our days around young children and having to bear the weight of responsibility mean that when we get to relinquish our roles for a night, we show just how young at heart we are. Yes, I've suffered a few bouts of embarrassment from staff parties gone by, and I've watched as some of my more experienced and esteemed colleagues have done some outrageous things that I wouldn't have expected from respected members of the local community… but, hey, you only live once.

Your school's social calendar depends on how your school 'does things' and whether your colleagues enjoy the opportunity to go out together. I've seen some schools where staff just go out for Christmas and the end of the academic year, and others where Ofsted inspections, assessment weeks and finishing off a round of parents' evenings are cause for celebration. In fact, in one of my old schools, we enjoyed a weekly 'Pub Friday' at the village local to celebrate the end of the working week.

Why, you might ask, have I chosen to write a chapter about this? Well, there are two reasons: partly to warn you how a night out with teachers can really be, but mostly to tell you that this is another great opportunity to get to know people in your school and build some bridges.

I am quite a shy person, so it took a lot of courage for me to get involved with any social occasions, but I soon came to realise that I worked with a brilliant, fun and supportive bunch of people and this was the time and place to see their true selves, beyond the friendly faces I already saw at work. During my first staff night out, I had some lovely comments from TAs who wanted me to know that I was doing a good job, a member of the SLT bought me a drink to say 'well done' for a great first term, and I spent nearly an hour having an actual conversation with a teaching assistant who had been working with me for a morning every week but whom I'd never had time to speak with. Teaching is not an easy profession, so in many schools your colleagues become like a little second family. My advice is just to make sure that you don't end up going too far during a night out and doing something that gets you into trouble or causes upset. It isn't like in the sitcoms, where you can avoid people and hide at your desk all day.

Oh, and if you think that these occasional high-jinks make us any less professional – rubbish! We used to have an Inset day in London once every two years, and we all looked forward to going into the city when it came around. It was here that we always realised how we were surrounded by 'suits' and people from every industry and role. We teachers might not get as much of a chance to get out on the town, but when we do, we do.

If you think I am going to be telling you how to link a staff night out with your Teachers' Standards, you couldn't be further from the truth. No one wants to see any evidence!

Top tips and tricks

1. Socialise – a staff social is a chance to chill and chat with everyone. I always spend some time with my year team and my friends but make a point of talking with as many people as I can. Also, don't be suckered into playing 'avoid the headteacher'; go and have a quick chat.

2. Double-check the details. Make sure you know where and when the event is, as well as checking what it is. Dressing to impress is good for a three-course sit-down dinner, but not as good for axe-throwing and a beer festival.

3. Plan your way home. I'm not trying to parent anyone, but make sure you know how to get back. Maybe you can share a ride with a colleague who lives close by, or someone can pick you up. If you are using public transport, check when it comes and when the last service is. Long story short, don't be the one stranded at the end of the night because you're new and you've lost track of time! We don't need stories of Cinderella and her pumpkin.

4. Find the balance. I admit to having had staff nights out when I've enjoyed being 'out out' and nights when it tiptoed a bit too far (never led by me, I promise!). Keep an eye on what you're drinking, and save yourself from any embarrassment when you get back to school.

5. Enjoy it. Aside from all the practical advice, make the most of the chance to let your hair down and unwind. You work incredibly hard, and you deserve it!

18 The work–life balance

I tutted as I walked out the front door of the school. It was 6.00 pm on a Friday, and I was last out again. I'd seen my mentor leaving at 3.30 pm and the last of my year team at 4.00 pm. I'd got a text a few minutes later asking if I was coming to the pub before heading home. My response was two-thirds true: 'Heading home now to get some rest. I'm shattered! See you Monday.' For some reason, I just hadn't had my head in the game that week, and despite my usual 55 hours on the front line, I was behind. I'd be taking 90 books home that weekend, and as I loaded the big blue box on to the front seat, I was frustrated to have not relieved myself of the burden.

When I pulled out the gate, my phone rang, and a photo of my mum and dad popped up on the screen, making me smile.

I answered on speakerphone and could hear my parents, with my brother in the background. Their weekend had started already.

'You still coming down this weekend?'

'Wish I could, Mum. I have so much work to do, and if I don't, next week is just going to be a nightmare. I'll give you a call on Sunday.'

'That's all right. We'll see you soon. I know you're busy. Just make sure you get some rest this weekend, all right?'The worried maternal tone came through as Mum replied, and I could hear my dad's concern without him even speaking.

'I will, Mum. Promise. Love you!'

'Love you,' the trio chimed back before I disconnected their call.

I slumped into my seat and cried. Pure guilt swept over me. I was prioritising work over my family, and by Monday morning no one would even realise how much I'd put into getting everything done. When I got back to my flat, I left the box in the car and went inside. A headache was brewing, and I decided time in bed was better than anything else at that moment.

I might as well have been hungover on Saturday morning – I felt that run-down. My head was still pounding, my eyes were sore and my body just felt overwhelmed with aches and pains. What I needed was some TLC and time to rest and recover. I needed to step away from the workload and focus on myself, or Monday-morning me was going to be a mess. I dragged myself up, showered, dressed and jumped in the car, moving the big blue box into the boot.

An hour later, I arrived at my parents' place in Portsmouth. It finally felt like a weekend. The family was surprised but happy to see me. Mum gave me a tight hug and Dad got the kettle straight on. For lunch, I drove us down to the seafront to blow the cobwebs away and get some chips. We went shopping to get the supplies for a barbecue and a roast, so that Mum would know I was going back well fed. The four of us laughed, chatted, ate, drank and relaxed – it was just what I needed.

Driving home late on Sunday evening, the image of the big blue box came flooding back, and I realised I wouldn't be getting to bed that side of midnight. I could feel myself tensing up again and feeling guilty that I had enjoyed myself instead of working. Arriving at the flat, I went to the boot. I picked up my weekender, but decided to leave the books behind. The weekend was for me. I would just have to catch up during the week.

Monday came, and the big blue box of books finally left the car. They hadn't been marked, but they'd travelled 150 miles over the weekend and experienced the sights, sounds and smells of the seaside. More importantly, so had I. As it was, the children marked their own maths, and a surprise hour of PPA on Monday afternoon meant I was all caught up before leaving at 6.00 pm all over again. It turned out I could fit in some 'me time' after all.

I couldn't write a book for new teachers and not talk about finding the balance between your work and your life outside of school. It is something that is discussed a lot in staffrooms, by education unions and in the wider world of wellbeing – and, honestly, it's something I struggled with for a long time before eventually managing to juggle the two, which changed my outlook and career completely.

The definition of having a good work–life balance is different for each of us. For me, I've realised that it's about making sure that I give my best to my job (and my pupils), while securing enough time and energy to give my best to myself. Notice how neither of them get 'my all', because it's OK not to do that – this was where my first mistake stemmed from. As a person, I throw myself into whatever project I am working on, so when I first stepped into the classroom as a teacher, it became my one and only focus. I would spend pretty much every hour that the building was open in my classroom and would take home a list to work through until I went to bed. I was disappointed to be stifled by a school that locked the front door at 6.00 pm, knowing that I could be so much more productive at my desk, with my resources to hand. Weekends would be filled with marking and planning, while invitations to see friends were often cancelled and visits to family were later regretted when I realised what hadn't been done in that time. Dinners were quick to cook and eat, my social life was non-existent and I wasn't looking after my body or my mind. Luckily, an intervention came soon after.

One morning in late October, I arrived at work and signed in at my usual 7.00 am. As I did so, a fellow early riser said good morning, but, unusually, she called me into her office. It was my deputy head. She'd noticed I was working 7.00–6.00 every day and had started to spot the signs of exhaustion plastered on my face. She didn't tell me that she'd clocked my workaholism, but instead asked how I was faring. She checked whether I was managing to prioritise what was important and letting some of the optional tasks go. I admitted that I wasn't. We spoke more about her experiences and the importance of looking after ourselves as teachers. I later realised I'd left her office with an improved outlook, because instead of being annoyed about the loss of work time, I recognised that I could have spent those 30 minutes in bed this morning or used them to have a proper breakfast, not a cereal bar at the photocopier.

After that, the balance slowly reset itself, but it was a slow process. Some weeks I would still hit the 55-hour mark and still have a million things to do as I chased deadlines; other weeks would include the occasional spare hour for me to get home early, go for a walk and catch up on some telly. The weekend that opened this chapter came at the end of November, while I was still coming to terms with accepting that teaching didn't have to dictate every waking minute. I also found that what the work–life balance looked like changed from week to week and depended on what season it was, what was going on at work and how I was feeling. The key to success was listening to what I needed first and foremost, meaning that I could be on top form to give my class my best.

If you feel you are struggling to find that balance, my advice is to talk to someone about it: your ECT mentor, a work colleague, a teacher friend (non-teachers don't always get it), a family member or someone you trust. Be honest with them and yourself. They might hold a solution, a time-saving tip or the knowledge that will save you. Sometimes, tasks take twice as long when you don't know an easier way to do them, or when you insist on always giving your all instead of giving enough.

Another piece of advice is not to be drawn into the toxic thought that staying at work for hours and hours is a badge of honour. I have met and worked with quite a few teachers who would proudly proclaim that they averaged 60 hours a week before going home to do more work. This can make others feel guilty for getting their work done in less time, or make them question whether they are pulling their weight. If you consistently find yourself being first in and last out or spending more than 50 hours a week at work, the truth is you are likely doing something ineffectively – and it's all right to admit that. I might just be words in a book at this point, but I truly don't want to see any of my fellow teachers burning out and breaking down. I've seen it first hand, and let me tell you, it isn't pretty.

I make no apologies for this chapter being more personal and less positive than the others. That's because the side effects of not having a healthy work–life balance can be detrimental and disastrous to you as a teacher and as a person. You matter more than your job. Don't give your all; give your best.

Top tips and tricks

1. Schedule in 'me time'. Commit to spending time looking after yourself by putting it into the diary. Do something fun, go somewhere exciting, meet someone you care about or just catch up on rest!

2. Get advice about your workload. Be confident in asking your mentor, your year team or a senior leader to clarify any tasks that you think are taking you too long. Ask if they can show you how they'd do it or clarify whether what you've already done is enough.

3. Timings aren't just for children. As new teachers, we are always told to give times to each part of a lesson; I found that giving myself a timeframe for a set of books or a piece of paperwork helped keep me focused and pacy.

4. Learn to prioritise. Decide which tasks need to be done first and which ones are essential. This will help you feel less time pressure when deadlines loom closer and will let you discard some of the tasks you would like to do but don't really need to.

5. Know that giving your best doesn't mean giving your all. Give what you want and give what you can, but remember that a burned-out teacher isn't going to have any great impact. Your class would rather have you on good form than on edge and struggling to cope.

19 Running a club

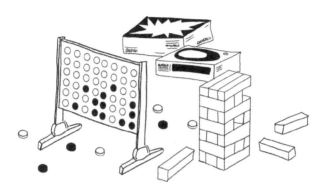

'5… 4… 3… 2… 1…'

'Welcome to our brand-new school podcast! On our first episode, we'll be discovering the school's favourite subjects and interviewing our teachheader…'

Laughter erupted from the children sitting around the classroom as I chuckled along with our junior presenter.

'Let's take that from the top again, shall we? Quiet, everyone!'

The others in the staffroom had said that I was mad for wanting to run Radio Club as my entry into our clubs offering. The thing is, our headteacher insists that it is school policy for all teachers, even new ones, to run a weekly club, and after a scarring experience in the autumn term I felt like it was time for something different and less dangerous. What had been my original offering? A high-octane, high-risk and highly dangerous group known as Board Games Club.

You may laugh, but it turned out that our weekly gatherings should probably have had a risk assessment, considering the number of injuries sustained. I might have expected it from some of the more sporty offerings; there were always a couple of children coming in from hockey or football with grazes needing wet paper towels or bumps requiring ice packs – but board games? Those were safe, right? Wrong!

After the missing dice incident in September that caused a sickening bang and impressive 'head egg' for a Year 4 pupil, and the case of the bad loser in October that saw a snakes-and-ladders game trashed (with a projectile counter narrowly missing a pupil's eye), I was hoping that things would quieten down as we approached Christmas. It turns out the now-famous 'pawn problem' of November would quash that hope. I remember little Steven coming up to me, quiet but panicked, while I was trying to show a couple of Year 6 pupils how to play Ludo. He tugged at my sleeve and attempted to get my attention.

'Everything OK, Steven?' I asked while keeping my eyes on the game at hand. No answer. Just another tug on the sleeve.

'What's up?' Again, no answer. I gave in and let my focus leave Ludo.

'Steven! How did you…?'

My shriek wasn't of anger, but of shock and concern. How did a Year 3 pupil end up with a chess pawn lodged into his left nostril? His eyes were watering more now as he realised the severity of the situation. He tried giving the piece a little pull, but it was stuck tight. I knew I should keep my cool, but I didn't know how I was going to explain this one to his parents.

Long story short, Steven was fine after the brave soldier was dislodged from its new battlefront, but the club was soon disbanded. I decided to go for something safer. Radio Club was born and, as a result, I was excited to share some of my own skills and passions with the children. Surely that was what clubs were all about anyway…

I admit that I don't have enormous enthusiasm for my club every Wednesday lunchtime (particularly if I'm reliving a harrowing board game-related injury), but I recognised early on that providing pupils with experiences outside of the curriculum is excellent for them. In fact, for some children, it's what they look forward to most in the week, encouraging them to come to school far more than normal lessons do. All of that means I don't mind our school's mandatory policy of teachers giving up their time to run a club, because I understand the difference it can make.

The Social Mobility Commission, an advisory public body of the DfE, said in a 2019 report:

> Extracurricular activities give young people the confidence to interact socially with others, extend their social networks beyond existing friendship groups, and provide them with new skills and abilities. Some also perceive them as important for their long-term career aspirations as well as useful in building stronger university and job applications.

I can say, hand on heart, that I agree. I've loved getting to work with children from across the year groups and forging the chance for them to work together; give the younger pupils the chance to work with the older ones, and vice versa, and they will take it! Depending on the range of clubs your school has (which you could help to widen with your choice), your pupils could pick up some new skills and abilities. I've seen chess clubs teaching strategy and patience, gardening clubs getting children outdoors and getting their green fingers dirty, eco councils appreciating and acting for their environment, science clubs pushing the boundaries of the subject in schools, language clubs building resilience alongside vocabulary and confidence, and even a walking club promoting the importance of exercise and wellbeing. All these skills and traits can be invaluable to the children we teach and could give them the edge later in life. The thought of my little Radio Club potentially helping a past pupil on a UCAS application one day makes me smile.

More than anything, running a club can be another chance to put a bit of you into your school community and to get the opportunity to weave some of what matters to you into your workday. Not many jobs can offer that. Just no nap clubs, OK?

Organising and running a club can give you some strong evidence for certain Teachers' Standards.

Standard		Evidence
1	High expectations	What better way to inspire, motivate and challenge pupils than providing something exciting and unique that interests them? Alongside fostering new skills and knowledge, clubs are brilliant for building mutual respect and demonstrating positive attitudes, values and behaviour.
5	Adaptive teaching	Club meetings may not be lessons, but you are still teaching! Adapting your session content for the benefit of your pupils, their prior experience, their strengths and any additional needs is just what you do in a maths or English lesson, so why not use it as evidence here too?

Standard		Evidence
8	Professional behaviours	This standard could come from your positive contribution to the school's extra-curricular offer or working with people in your wider community. Both are great examples of Teachers' Standard 8 and could be easily evidenced by running a club.

Top tips and tricks

1. Choose something you feel passionate about. If you're running a club based on something you like, it becomes less of a chore. If your passion is accessible for the age group you teach, the world is your oyster.

2. Schedule it mindfully. I chose Wednesday lunchtime for my club because I had PPA all Wednesday afternoon. Try to avoid days when you have break duty or late-finishing meetings. You could even share a club with a colleague if there's no good time to have it, so you alternate and share the load.

3. Consider budget and practicality. I was lucky to have a home studio that I could pinch microphones, headphones and my laptop from, but if you need lots of expensive resources or a huge space for your activity, think about whether it will work. You don't want to be footing a large bill for supplies and making your bursar think you've gone too far.

4. Share what you've achieved. When your club produces or wins something, spread the word. You could add photos to the newsletter, get some space on the school website or ask if your new creation could be displayed somewhere. We used to publish our podcasts on the school website once every half term.

5. Get your community involved. Working in a school of more than 300 children meant I had access to more than 500 parents and an amazing local community with an abundance of skills and knowledge (in my case, including two radio presenters and two TV presenters!). Ask around for relevant people willing to visit for a Q&A session or even co-run the club with you. Remember that safeguarding must take priority – clear it with your SLT and speak to your school office about the necessary paperwork and checks.

20 Cake sales

The school bell echoed across the empty playground. We braced ourselves. A low rumble started drawing closer, and I could have sworn the ground started shaking. Hundreds of hungry pupils, desperate parents and determined childminders raced across the playground from every angle. I felt for the dogs being dragged in tow – poor things.

All that stood between us and the stampede was a couple of plastic tables and the cakes kindly donated by parents of my class. There was a mix of cakes and biscuits, traybakes and muffins, homemade and shop-bought… no shame here; every contribution was going to raise much-needed money for a local animal shelter that the children had voted to support during a recent PSHE lesson. (Trust me, it's always the animals that win.)

No sooner had the first customer reached our makeshift stall than a ravenous rabble was surrounding us on all sides. Frantic hands were thrusting sticky money at us (obviously hoping to buy a second cake), and the noise was something else. There were children buying four cakes for themselves and a mum of four haggling with me to buy her kids one cake each (I was generous and went with '4 for the price of 3'). I felt like some sort of celebrity amid the hubbub, with people shouting my name and wanting my attention – but not for a photo; it was all for a slice of Victoria sponge or a chocolate-chip cookie.

Fifteen minutes passed, and I could breathe a sigh of relief along with the children who had managed to cope with the onslaught; we had lost one who'd forgotten they had a swimming lesson after school, and another couldn't handle the stress of quick arithmetic. It was worthwhile though. With the coins counted, we had raised around £100 for the local shelter, and I'd bought myself a Bakewell to go with my cuppa.

I'll reason with you – a cake sale isn't a staple in a new teacher's calendar or career. But it was something that stuck out for me from my first year in the classroom. Why? Well, not only was it an experience to witness a stampede the likes of which I'd never see if I was handing out homework, but it was also a chance to participate in another side of what happens in my school and something that my children felt passionate about. Genuine thought and enthusiasm went into the PSHE session when I let my class consider who was worthy of our soon-to-be-received gains. We had pitches from more than 20 different causes, most of which were linked to a story from the children's short-but-significant lives so far. I almost cried over a few, especially when Wan told us about his aunt, who had recently been diagnosed with breast cancer. To hear an eight-year-old speaking so maturely and convincingly about why he wanted the money to help those who are also suffering brought a tear of sorrow and pride to my eye. Unfortunately for him, as I said, he lost to the usually triumphant animal charity choice.

There were quite a few events over my first year that brought me the same sort of insight into my pupils and the community I was serving: our enterprise week (where each class had £30 to buy resources, design and make products and sell them for profit), our 'choose your own topic' week and our citizenship week. All of these gave the children the chance to choose their cause, explore their own thinking and fight their case. It clued me in to what was important to the people in my area and demonstrated how I could pull on my pupils' passions to tailor my teaching and get them motivated. All of that from what charity they'd choose to support or what they wanted to do with our £30 budget.

More than that, a cake sale is another opportunity for you as a teacher to get your face out there and be seen by families across the school. It always pays to be known for the right reasons around the school, and while we don't need to be friends with the children or the parents, any popularity can be beneficial. You might wonder why this is a priority when you are already having to manage the communications with and expectations of 30 families, but it pays to get to know as many people as you can. After all, you will be getting a new class eventually.

In terms of Teachers' Standards, there are no prizes for guessing which this situation can help you evidence.

Standard		Evidence
8	Professional behaviours	Once again, you're clocking up opportunities to contribute to your wider school ethos and be part of the community. Any records of your participation would be good evidence here.

Top tips and tricks

1. Seek out opportunities to get involved. I could easily sound like a stuck record with this tip, but it's so valuable: make the most of these chances to show your face for 15 minutes and experience the other sides of our job (not just the bit at the whiteboard).

2. Get to know other families. Being on the playground or at the cake stall means you are visible to people outside of your class. If you plan on sticking around at your school, this is only ever a good thing!

3. Use fundraising to your advantage. One of the many great things about being a teacher is that if you are trying to raise money for something, you have a platform to do so. When one of my previous colleagues needed sponsorship to swim the English Channel, we had a couple of cake sales and events, which easily raised the thousands they needed.

4. Show interest in your class events. This is a prime way to ensure you are building that rapport with your pupils and their families. Plus, I promise it feels good to be part of the class community.

5. Take a couple of quid. Don't just sell cakes, buy some for yourself! You'll be a few minutes behind on your marking by the time you get back to your classroom, so help the cause and buy something to go with your cuppa.

21 Half terms

It's long been a tradition of mine to designate any day or week signifying the point of being 'halfway there' with the name of Bon Jovi, so, as we reached the final Friday of February (well, the last one in school, anyway), we celebrated with 'Bon Jovi Day' being written as the date on the board and a rip-roaring rendition of 'Livin' on a Prayer' to end the day. We were indeed halfway through the spring term and halfway to summer.

Three days later and Monday had rolled around again, but there was something very special about waking up on a Monday and seeing the clock saying that it was 9.00 am. Normally, I'd skip a heartbeat – and I admit I did my usual panicked check on the school website to make sure I had the day right – but the truth was precious: it was half term, and I didn't have to be anywhere. There were plenty of places I'd have liked to be, and plenty of plans in place, but there was nowhere I had to be, and that made the difference.

I decided to celebrate my first half year of teaching with a mini tour of all of my favourite haunts – back down to Portsmouth to see the family, a few catch-ups with friends at various bars, a trip up to London to be a tourist for a day and, of course, plenty of evenings in by myself to relax and make the most of the peace and quiet that a lack of children brought. The ringing in my ears was slowly disappearing. I had nine mornings without an alarm (absolute bliss!), stayed up past my 'bedtime' and let my body detox itself from the caffeine that usually powered me through term time. Yes, half term was like a spa retreat for life, but without having to go anywhere, and it was just what I needed.

By Friday, I felt revitalised, and, while I had decided that this was the day that I'd dedicate to getting my plans and resources in order for the new half term, I had no regrets about choosing to do that work while settling down on the sofa. No, I could get used to working with a hot chocolate in hand, sitting next to my big sunny window with some classical music on the speaker. It was like Christmas had come early… or a few weeks too late. I found myself powering through the plans, snacking on a biscuit or two after each one and being far more productive than I would have been during my usual lunch break.

However, with all my new-found appreciation of being away from school, what I didn't expect was the feeling that arrived on Saturday evening: a strange sense of being ready to go back to work. It was far from the dread I was expecting to come on Sunday, and I definitely wasn't looking forward to getting up at 6.00 am every weekday again, but it was humbling to know that I was missing my job, missing my classroom and missing the children. Maybe teaching was the correct career choice for me after all.

As we reach the halfway point of the school year (and the book!), it's time to be frank about the school holidays, or 'holidays'. According to the School Teachers' Pay and Conditions Document, we lovely lot are in school for the equivalent of 39 working weeks a year (38 spent with the children and the other week made up of Inset days), and this means that we have 13 weeks away from the classroom every academic year. Unfortunately, anyone who isn't a teacher counts these weeks as time when our minds are completely out of the classroom, but this often isn't the case. My family and friends always laugh at me when a shopping trip or a walk out and about becomes an idea for a lesson or resource. It's a curse, and it's real!

Half terms and holidays are times that you should use to recuperate from the stress and strain of term time. We may not be saving lives, but we are shaping minds, minds that might one day be saving lives, making laws, keeping us moving, cleaning our environments, stacking shelves, designing inventions and contributing to our future. That matters, and it isn't easy. Having a break is brilliant, and it lets us get off the treadmill for a minute and take a breather.

However, it is often the case that you will have tasks to get ready for the next leg of the marathon. As I mentioned, I love doing some of my work during the break because I can do it in peace and at my own pace. I set aside a day of the week to work through the planning, paperwork and 'to do' lists, while some of my teacher friends prefer to do an hour or two each day and yet others will use a couple of mornings; regardless of how you split up your time, make sure you get everything prepared so that you can return ready and raring to go. Oh, and if you've booked a holiday away for the whole time (which we've all done, and why shouldn't you?), then make sure you use the last couple of weeks before the break to get prepared. Again, it just dilutes that stark shock when you return on a Monday morning.

Finally, before the real tips and tricks for getting the most of your half terms and other 'holidays', a quick bit of advice, from me to you: if you see or hear somebody complaining about the time off that teachers get, or the 'easy ride' we have in our profession (or, as I've seen before, someone telling us we don't deserve to be considered 'professionals' with how simple our job is), just remember that many children in the world are not fortunate enough to kick-start their lives with a school education, and most of those who aren't lucky enough are wishing and praying that they could be in a classroom. None of that would be possible without teachers, and I can guarantee that every single one of those people airing their opinion (which they are entitled to, of course) went to school and benefitted from some of the incredible teachers who've gone before us. Avoid the conflict and the confrontation in the papers and on social media; remember that you are fantastic, valuable and worthy – we all are.

Top tips and tricks

1. Assess the situation before the break: what work do you have that you need to get done during half term? Check and make the list early on, because there's nothing worse than starting a new half term panicking about a crucial deadline you missed.

2. Plan things to do. While it's tempting to sit and do nothing for nine days (and I won't judge if you do), try to relish the chance to get out and about during

the break. Organise a catch-up with a friend or a walk somewhere local, or push the boat (or car) out and go for a day trip. I always find it makes the time away from work seem longer and makes me more relaxed.

3. Don't overdo it. Conversely to the previous point, try not to fill every day with wall-to-wall activities. Teaching is a lot more strenuous than people realise! A few late starts and an evening on the sofa can do wonders to relax the body and mind.

4. Listen to your body. For some reason, my body reacts to every single school break as if it is allergic to them; I always catch the bug or cold that I've been fending off in term time. For this reason, listen to what your body needs and respond accordingly to gear up for the next stint.

5. If you are a night owl – one of those who is naturally late to bed – try to keep your check-in time in the Land of Nod reasonable. This used to be a problem for me, and I found it tough getting back into the routine come Sunday night.

22 Exams

It felt somewhat surreal after we had transformed the room into 'test mode'. Tables were split apart, chairs were moved to the ends and papers were delivered, all while pencils were feverishly sharpened to within an inch of their lives. I remembered vividly how I'd sat nervously at tables just like these. My mind went back to being in Year 6, when I'd sat the Standard Attainment Tests (SATs, or 'Silly Assessment Tests', as we now call them in my class to lighten the mood). My teachers had done a great job of quashing anxieties, but we knew we'd arrived at the moment that the last four years had been geared towards. Since then, no matter if it was a mock or an exam, I always knew I had to give my best and felt immense pressure to do so. Those flashbacks brought out a surreal sense of unrest in me, because this time

I was seeing it from the other perspective. It may have just been the Year 4 mid-year tests, but I couldn't tell who was more worried about the outcomes: me or the children!

'Keep in mind what I've said since the winter break,' I told them. 'It doesn't matter what your final score is. I just want your very best. If you can tell me in an hour that you gave this paper your all, then I don't mind whether you get one or one hundred marks. Just do yourself proud. Oh, and check your work!' The final comment lightened the air with laughter as the pupils recalled my impression of a child 'checking their work' by picking up a paper and looking in its general direction for a couple of seconds before asking if they can go to the toilet.

I didn't want my children to be apprehensive about having to tackle these tests, because while it was an indicator for them of how they were doing, it was really for me and for the school. The last thing they needed before trying to focus independently for an hour in silence was butterflies in their tummies.

'Right. It's 9.45 am. You've got this. Good luck. One hour. Off you go.' I sat down at my desk and slurped my tea. The only downside of being the teacher now was the boredom of the hour to come. There was nothing I could do during a reading paper…

For some children, assessments are the best bit of the year, but for others it will be their worst nightmare. The same can be said for us as teachers, because while our pupils' test results should only signpost the learning journey and show us what we need to work on with our classes, they can often influence our appraisals and success in schools (although, as teaching unions always argue, they shouldn't).

Exams, assessments and tests – whatever you call them – are a big part of our profession and are somewhat controversial in the world of primary education. Anyone with any exposure to the world of primary schools during the past few decades will be aware of SATs. These exams came about after the landmark Education Reform Act 1988, which was the birthplace of key stages and the first National Curriculum. The act led to the introduction of the Key Stage 1 SATs and Key Stage 2 SATs in the 1990s, both of which evolved into the annual assessments that Year 2 and Year 6 pupils sit now. The original concept? A way of assessing pupils consistently across the country, so that teachers and parents could accurately see how their children stacked up against the nation, schools could see how they were performing in terms of attainment and progress and the government (along with any other interested parties) could rank and rate schools based on their results. It removed subjectivity and inconsistency between establishments from the equation, meaning that accurate data could be used to quantify what had previously been virtually unquantifiable. The idea was a success, and assessments in the primary sector were here to stay, although the yearly science assessments for all become biennial and were sat by only a proportion of pupils in some schools, creating a sampling test to support teacher assessments.

As time has gone on and the landscape has developed, more exams and tests have been introduced by the DfE (and its various aliases) to the primary key stages, as a way of monitoring performance and progress across the nation. Year 1 pupils now sit an annual phonics screening check, and a yearly multiplication tables check is now administered for all Year 4 pupils. There is also a baseline assessment completed in Reception to give an early starting point for future measurements, working alongside the early years foundation stage profiles.

Now, I am not going to dip any toes into the politics pond, but I will say one thing. Regardless of your opinions on how national assessments form part of pupils' learning journeys, it is important we acknowledge that our pupils need to be prepared to be tested more now than ever before. As a new teacher, this can be quite tough, especially if you are feeling the pressure yourself and believe that the resulting data could reflect poorly on your teaching. I remember, in my first assessment week as a teacher, seeing how badly my class had scored on their reading paper. I knew I'd tried my hardest to boost their skills and knowledge, but it didn't seem enough. Once the papers were marked, I was petrified that I'd lose my job because my class hadn't made progress in their first term. I was sure I had to be to blame. As it was, yes, I reflected on my practice and realised what more I could have been doing to help my children, but my mentor helped me see that the cold bug that had been going around during test week, the step up from their previous Year 3 papers and the fact we hadn't covered the whole curriculum in the first two half terms meant we were always going to be on the back foot. Luckily for me, things were the same for the other classes in the year group. Always seek context for your results and look at the bigger picture.

So, what can we do to prepare our pupils and make the most of the exams we have in primary schools? Well, it helps to remind children that tests aren't going to change their lives. I have often said to my classes that exams are a bit like dentists: their job is to find holes to fill and fix before they get worse (although most people don't like dentists either!). It's about gaining insight from analysing the results so that we can use them to springboard ourselves into the next phase, finding our way through the busy syllabuses and curriculum so that we can get to the finish line together.

Assessments have their own Teachers' Standard, so there are no surprises about Standard 6 being important here.

Standard		Evidence
2	How pupils learn	Arguably you can't promote good progress without testing and assessments. Being accountable for your pupils' performance is demonstrated through effective use of test results to inform what you plan and teach next. Evidence of how you guide your pupils to improvement, directed by their previous assessment data, will work well for Teachers' Standard 2.
5	Adaptive teaching	Alongside recognising the holistic and personal strengths and needs of pupils, you can use testing to uncover the academic side that must be considered. If you see any trends in the data across a class or for a group of children, you can use these to inform and promote a new approach through your teaching.
6	Assessment	As this standard indicates, accurate and productive use of assessment is the name of the game. By marking tests, recording the data and analysing it to monitor progress, you are ticking most boxes for Teachers' Standard 6. Evidence this by showing copies of your data, any references to results in your future planning and examples of analysis you've completed.

1. Get everything prepared in advance to alleviate some of the fuss and chaos before the test. Have you got the right equipment and the correct number of papers? Check you have the correct papers too – I once had 20 Year 4 reading papers mixed up with 10 Year 5 papers without realising. You could get the children to move their tables in advance too, providing a quick brain break and a few minutes to decompress.

2. Don't cheat. There's no value in giving the children the answers or helping them too much. Yes, it's tempting sometimes (especially when a child is frustratingly close), but it doesn't benefit them, you or the future teachers they go on to.

3. Mark what you can. While some schools will ask TAs or supporting adults to mark papers, I make a point of marking each one myself. As the teacher, it gives me more satisfaction and a better knowledge of each learner as I see the story of their test paper first hand. Plus, it means I have a much better awareness ahead of any tracking or parent meetings.

4. Don't be defeated. If the data doesn't go your way, remember that it only provides a snapshot of one time on one day. Use it as a motivator and an indicator to kick-start the learning, especially as that's what it's truly for anyway.

5. Celebrate successes. Make sure you and your class enjoy the achievements and little moments in assessment weeks. In my class, we cheer the ending of each countdown timer, applaud anyone who feels proud of their work after finishing a test (regardless of their performance) and pinpoint those who've used their test skills well. During mocks and midterms, I even wander around and pick a few impressive answers to share after we're done.

23 Residential trips

It may have been 1.00 am, but even in my sleep-deprived state the irony of the situation wasn't lost on me. When I was young, I was always the child on a residential who wouldn't sleep, would get homesick, would cry and would want my parents to collect me early. A couple of decades on, and there I was, being woken up by a knock on my door and the sound of sniffling sobs. After hitting my head on the bunk bed above mine, I stumbled to the door and found myself smiling as I realised how my old teachers would be laughing at me being in their shoes. As a non-parent, I had wondered before the trip how I'd manage with a crying child waking me up in the early hours, but I was proud to say afterwards that I thought I would make a good dad one day.

A couple of hours later, after failing to get back to sleep once I'd managed to convince the pupil to go back to bed and have another crack at sleeping, I was up and out. There was something very peculiar about waking on my first full day on a residential, because it was like nothing I'd experienced before as a grown up. I was thinking about it while drinking my first cup of tea of the day and watching the sunrise over Ashdown Forest. Normally, I woke up in my flat and had the morning to myself to get ready at my own pace and in my own space, but that day I was in a block with 130 students and staff, and the peace I was enjoying was soon to be dashed.

And dashed it was. By 7.30 am the corridors were alive with the sounds of chatter, excitement and the occasional stifled cry as more homesick pupils realised that they too weren't waking to their normal home comforts. Breakfast solved everything though. For me, it was a second cup of tea, a pastry and a sausage sandwich; it was all about the carbs, and I was obviously fuelling myself for a marathon that day.

A marathon turned out not to be too far off what the day felt like. It was brilliant to see my little day group enjoying themselves and being kids. The adults had all been saying over a hot chocolate the evening before that experiences like this were so important because they let the children have freedom to be children – something that seems to be lost more and more in the modern day. All they needed to shake off the shackles was to go orienteering through a forest, track some animal footprints through the mud, take part in some team challenges that showed just how shocking their teamwork really was, and wade through a cold muddy river on the search for 'drop bears'. I was humbled to hear laughter and could almost feel everyone's relief at just being able to focus on enjoying themselves.

The final activity of the day for my lot was abseiling. Setting off for the tower, I brought my fifth cup of tea with me and assumed a spot in the sunshine next to the bench where the awaiting abseilers sat. There were some nerves in the group, but I was proud to see them all supporting each other and demonstrating that kids just seem to be fearless. I'd always envied that. There was no way you'd get me jumping off the tower!

'Sir?' The instructor interrupted my train of thought as I finished my cup and sat back to get the best of the afternoon sun. 'Did you want to have a go?'

'No, I'm good, thank you. Appreciate you asking though.'

'Oh, Mr Pearce, please?'

'Remember how we said we wouldn't force you to do anything you didn't want to do, Suni? Well, the same goes for us adults!'

I was quite impressed with myself for spinning that around so quickly and convincingly. There wasn't a chance I was going up there. I looked up, confirming my reluctance, but my group were chanting my name louder and louder, testing my resolve. You teach your classes not to give in to peer pressure, but they sure can dish it out.

Five minutes later, I was standing forty feet up, knees knocking, sweat pouring from my hands, trussed up like a turkey.

'They'll love you for doing this, sir,' the instructor assured me as she quadruple-checked the carabiner at my request.

'They might love me, but I don't love them. Maths test on Monday, that's for sure.' We both laughed, and I took a deep breath, put on a fake smile and did my best SAS impression over the side… all without swearing in front of the kids.

We have already had a chapter about school trips in this book, but if you are lucky enough to go on a residential trip during your first year, you're in for a great experience – but, I warn you, you'll probably come home feeling like you've done three weeks on 'I'm a Teacher, Get Me Out of Here'. I'll admit that being away from your home comforts and being 'on duty' for 24 hours a day is quite an intense and overwhelming experience sometimes. However, those moments when the exhaustion overcomes you for a minute or two are enormously outweighed by the rewards of an adventure like this.

When it comes to finding the value of residential trips, I must mention a past programme that provides us with a wealth of knowledge and a rationale for why learning away from the classroom is a real benefit for primary pupils. The Paul Hamlyn Foundation collected impact statements from 60 schools and published the report 'Learning Away' in 2015. Its advisor Tim Brighouse said, 'For some children a week's residential experience is worth more than a term of school. We know we want it for our own children – we need to make sure other people's children experience it too.' The benefits aren't limited to academic impacts from children learning through focused experiential opportunities: the report says that 75 per cent of primary pupils admitted that they got on better with other pupils in the class after a residential, 58 per cent of pupils (up to Key Stage 5) felt that their behaviour in school was better after a trip, and 23 per cent of parents recognised that their children's attendance improved once they'd returned from a residential trip. Personally, I hold up my hands and say that residential trips were invaluable for my pupils developing the values and qualities that we endeavour to establish in them; I have lost count of the times that a child has shown me resilience like never before, gained confidence to finally peek out of their shell and demonstrated respect for their peers when before they may not have given them the time of day. Taking everybody out of the comfort zones of the classroom and home is a genuine leveller, and it enables new opportunities for learning and personal growth.

Seeing pupils in a different environment is not only heart-warming and humbling for us as teachers but has a long-term impact. Again, the 'Learning Away' report says 82 per cent of teachers surveyed at the end of their project believed a residential trip 'made a significant or transformative impact on them seeing their students in a different light', and 78 per cent 'developed a better awareness of students' strengths and limitations' (Teachers' Standard 5, anybody?).

This chapter might feel slightly like a travel brochure, although your encounters with residential trips will be far from the 'holidays' that my colleagues and I have always jokingly called them. Nonetheless, I can advise wholeheartedly that if you are fortunate enough to get asked to go, you should seize the day! It will likely be one of the toughest and best moments of your first year.

Here's another good reason to give up your time – being part of a residential trip can be super evidence for your Teachers' Standards profile.

Standard		Evidence
1	High expectations	While this may seem like a strange standard to mention when you aren't in the classroom, residential trips are all about establishing a culture of positive attitudes and values so that everyone supports each other in challenging themselves.

Standard		Evidence
7	Managing behaviour	It shouldn't be a surprise that behaviour on a trip like this will be worlds apart from the behaviour in the classroom. Establishing clear rules, boundaries and expectations is important to ensure children can have fun and do so safely. If you're on a trip with instructors, you can get an insightful look at their strategies too.
8	Professional behaviours	If residential trips don't hit this standard, I don't know what does! Evidence of you taking part in a trip shows your commitment and contribution to the wider school community.

A packing list

Whilst tips and tricks are useful, what's more important is knowing what to pack for an excursion like this. Aside from the normal clothes and toiletries, here are some essentials to help you survive:

- Biscuits for your room – sustenance and a bit of a luxury!
- Sweets for your pocket – wine gums have always been my go-to for munching when out and about in the forest.
- Snacks for the evening – one year, we made the most of our post-bedtime daily debrief in the staffroom with crisps, brownies, sweets and even some cheese.

- Headphones – useful for some headspace in the evenings or overnight.

- Your favourite hot drink – some residential places will have tea or coffee, but for extra home comforts, take your own.

- Room spray or air freshener – if you're going to be staying in a dorm room for a couple of nights, it's nice to try and spruce it up a little.

- Cosy socks – useful when patrolling indoor areas.

- Sensible pyjamas – you don't know who might see you in them, after all.

- Pad and pen – I'm never without them, and they're always useful for lists or impromptu rotas.

- Portable charger – if you have phone signal when you're out and about, take a charger to ensure you have enough battery.

- Book or tablet – for entertainment in the evenings. If you're taking a tablet, get shows or films downloaded on it before you go, in case there is no Wi-Fi.

- Gloves – depending on when you go, these can be essential. Our Year 4 trip was at the end of February, and some years we went out in the snow.

- Wet wipes – useful for everything, especially if things aren't feeling fresh after a couple of days.

24 Class assemblies

I nodded to the two children by the computer, and they sprang into action.

'Here goes nothing,' I thought.

Two weeks previously, my year team had laughed at me when I'd revealed that I hadn't started thinking about my class assembly yet. I still had a few assessments to mark and a couple of meetings with parents who had missed their slots at the last parents evening, and I was exhausted after the residential trip. Honestly, the class assembly was the last thing on my mind. I was sure it wouldn't take that long to sort out anyway. It turned out those words would haunt me for the next fortnight as I realised how much hard work it could be to get a class assembly together.

I had naively thought that, just like with the Christmas concert, I could lead the class into the hall and get them to practise a few lines that they'd pick up easily. I was so very wrong. Luckily, I had my TA, who was obviously a class-assembly veteran, on hand. I was very quickly provided with a list of things to get sorted, including finding (or writing) a script, deciding on costumes, choosing music, making props, blocking out where people would sit, thinking about what would be on the screen and casting the different parts of the production. I wondered if I'd somehow stepped into Hollywood instead of my school that morning because, all of a sudden, 'executive producer' was another credit being added to the growing list of additional hats that a teacher has tucked away.

After a very late Monday evening and a couple of glasses of wine, everything was written (I'd decided to make the script my own for my first class assembly), and I revealed to the class the next morning that our assembly, scheduled for St. Patrick's Day, was going to be about patron saints and their stories. Why I hadn't focused it on the Romans unit we'd just finished in history I don't know! I had to laugh when the class's cheering was promptly followed by at least half of them admitting they didn't have a clue what a patron saint was. At least it meant that this would still be an educational experience for them, eh?

With sketches written, a song repurposed and a dance routine bubbling away as a work in progress, we could finally get underway. Despite tears from those who didn't get the main part they wanted, and more tears from those who didn't get to operate the computer, the following two weeks were relatively stress-free. Scripts went home that Tuesday afternoon, and from Wednesday onwards we ran through the lines twice a day, started each lesson with a rendition of our song and had a group of dancers practising on the playground every break time (their choice, not mine!). I might have misjudged how much effort it would be for me, and how much time we'd need, but I'd never underestimated the children's enthusiasm and excitement for the chance to perform to their parents and show the school what they'd been working on. That sense of pride and determination was so much greater than it would have been for a year group performance, because this was our class team pulling together to be the best we could be. It was lovely to see, and I was equally proud of them as young people as I was of their performances.

The day came around quickly, and on the afternoon of 17 March, 400 people sat in the hall, waiting for the show to begin. The headteacher delivered his usual routine of welcoming the parents, pointing out the exits and noting that we weren't due a fire drill that day. There was a mix of anticipation and nerves in the room, but I knew that the children would be fantastic. With introductions finished, it was our turn, and at the signal of a nod, we were off…

To this day, I am still incredibly proud of my pupils for pulling their class assembly out of the bag and proving that it can be done in nine school days. However, I have acted on hindsight and made sure to never leave it that late again! To do your class assembly justice and to stop sleepless nights, I'd recommend the same to you.

Some people say and believe that class assemblies aren't worth the loss of learning time, especially as you tend to sacrifice a few afternoons to repetitive rehearsals. Personally, I think that class assemblies are worthwhile, and they are something that I really miss when they are taken away (as they were during the COVID-19 pandemic). They provide pupils with an opportunity to develop new skills that don't get practised often in the curriculum and to learn some new facts (especially if it's about a topic not covered in class), and they act as another way of bridging the gap between the parents and us (but be prepared for tears if a parent isn't there when you're ready to go).

One of the greatest impacts of class assemblies that I have seen is how becoming an expert in a topic and then sharing it with others empowers my pupils to be proactive in their own learning and to take some ownership. A couple of years after my patron-saints offering, I worked with another class on an assembly about a solar eclipse that was due to happen midway during our show (I know, the timing was incredibly lucky when it came to finding a topical theme to focus on). My class of Year 4 children were so motivated by the fact that we'd get to show a real phenomenon happening in space during our assembly that they were doing research at home to find out more information, designing pinhole projectors to allow our pupils to see the effects of the moon moving in front of the sun and even finding out the time of the point of greatest eclipse so that we could use the NASA livestream to link up with the darkness we'd see through the hall windows. I have never seen a class so interested in their learning, even when teaching space in Year 5, and I believe it came from the fact that I'd allowed the children to become experts and immerse themselves in the topic with the intention of them presenting their findings to their parents and the school. That, and the fact that they enjoyed singing 'Eclipse Funk', my version of the Bruno Mars and Mark Ronson hit that came out in the same year; in my head, it's always worth having a good song to fill a couple of minutes in your assembly.

Long story short, a class assembly can be a lot of effort and can take up learning time that could arguably be better spent focusing on the National Curriculum, but it's another experience in your children's school journey that is different, creates a bit of buzz and refreshes their motivation to learn. If you are worried about it deflecting their learning, use a topic or theme from a recent unit and you're likely to have plenty of pieces to share and show. Plus, above all else, a class assembly can tick off some evidence for your Teachers' Standards.

Standard		Evidence
1	High expectations	Don't be afraid to push your pupils to produce and perform at their best. Your assembly doesn't need to be a masterpiece, but it is a super opportunity to develop and stretch the children in your class. Plus, they will need to show resilience, teamwork and a lot of patience when waiting for their turn to speak.
3	Subject and curriculum	While this standard might not seem applicable for some assemblies, if you have gone for a theme that links to recent learning in your classroom, this will be essential! Make sure all the information is correct before getting the children to learn it. A copy of the script is sufficient evidence here.
7	Managing behaviour	If you have yet to practise your non-verbal behaviour strategies, this will be the perfect time to do so. When I had more than 400 people in the hall at my class assembly, including the parents of a child who was poking their friend standing next to them, it was time to demonstrate my ability to have clear rules and expectations, enforced through a teacher stare and a raised eyebrow.

Top tips and tricks

1. Remember that it's a process. Avoid my mistake, and give yourself plenty of time to get things ready. You will need to prepare your assembly before rehearsing begins.

2. Choose whether you want to write or recycle. It's up to you whether you want to create your own tailor-made assembly or choose one of the many you can find online. Think about how many roles you need and what the theme will be.

3. Give parents lots of notice. If your pupils need to bring in costumes, their parents will appreciate as much time as you can give them. I usually let those without costumes come in wearing their own clothes, so they don't miss out.

4. Ask children which parts they want. I have found it beneficial to ask the children what sort of role they would prefer to have and then keep a record of what they've said. One year, a child said they didn't want to speak, and their parents complained the next day that their child was only dancing and singing. They backed down after I showed them the slip that their child had completed.

5. Remember that the parents will love it. Whatever comes of the assembly, the parents will 'ooh' and 'ahh' at all the right places. It's their rare opportunity to see their pride and joy onstage, so they tend to come away happy (and sometimes crying).

25 Strike day

I had been dreading the announcement, but from the feeling in the staffroom and from chatter amongst my teacher friends I knew it was coming.

'Teachers have decided to strike, strengthening their calls for increases to their pay. Unions have balloted their members in the past few weeks and today, and we now have confirmation that several teaching unions will join together for a combined day of strike action.'

As a new teacher, I didn't know what to think about the strike, and I hadn't known which box to tick on the form a few weeks earlier. I hadn't been suffering for as long as some of my colleagues, and I was quite happy with my starting wage. It was a lot more than I'd earned through my time at uni! I knew there were other areas of the job and of the industry in general that were being considered too: workload, education, testing. I had opinions on them, sure, but I didn't feel anyone would listen to the new guy. Was I even entitled to an opinion? I sought the advice of my mentor, an experienced teacher who I knew would be honest with me. They explained that they'd hit the top of the pay scale a few years ago and that, for them, wanting to stay on the front line and in the classroom meant that they would have to accept staying on pretty much the same wage for the rest of their career, except for the occasional 1 per cent pay rise (gratefully received, but not very encouraging). They also reassured me, as did my headteacher and deputy, that every teacher had a voice that was valued, and that the fact I was the last one in the door didn't mean my say had any less gravitas than someone who had been in the classroom for thirty years.

I went home that evening and thought some more. I wanted to be a teacher for the long haul, but I knew that in 20 years' time I might be feeling very differently if I'd worked up the ladder within the first decade and sat stagnant for the next. At the same time, was money really my motivator? Besides, striking for the day would mean my class couldn't come to school, and I felt I'd be letting them down. A few parents had inadvertently informed me that they were disappointed at the prospect of the strike, so I knew they wouldn't be jumping to support our cause if I did indeed decide to join the picket line. I was torn, and having only been in school for six months, I was at odds about what to do. All I knew was that I wanted the best for my class. And maybe a happier, more valued and appreciated teacher might be able to give them more. I wanted to be able to focus on my pupils and not on red tape. I wanted to be able to push back on why we nationally assess children so often. I wanted to be able to bring to the public's attention how tough some schools find it to function on the budgets they have been allocated. With that in mind, I knew my position. I added my tick to the 'yes' box and posted my slip before I could change my mind. Teachers support each other, and my colleagues needed me right then.

We often hear about unions and strikes on the news, and, as disruptive as it can be, strike action can be worthwhile. I found the decision to strike incredibly tough, not because I lost a day's pay but because I didn't understand what impact my solitary decision could make. Why would the parents of my pupils or the public listen to me or even care? It turned out that they did care, because the issues were significant for their children. While I might have irritated them by creating the need to sort out childcare for an extra day, many parents later thanked me for standing up for the rights of their little ones; it wasn't about the pay for me, it was about raising awareness of the fact that we as teachers want to do our very best, but it isn't always possible to do that with barriers in our way.

Generally speaking, strikes are just one tiny part of what a union handles. Most of us in the profession know unions to be a valuable source of advice about all things teaching. They know our roles inside out and can skilfully relay our rights and responsibilities at the drop of a hat. If you are unsure about what you are entitled to or need help managing a tricky situation, a union will often give objective advice and steps that can support you in managing what is happening. Unions can also provide further assistance and basic legal advice should the need arise. Personally, I have talked with my union a few times through my career so far: for clarity on my employee rights when my school became an academy, for support when I was unhappy with how I was being treated by a senior leader and for advice when I started dating a colleague and things developed into a serious ongoing relationship (a plot twist that I won't be writing about further!). Every time, my teaching union was there to listen, provide independent and constructive advice and offer me whatever support it could.

Even more importantly, teaching unions are there to 'shape the future of education', as the National Education Union (NEU) said when it formed in 2017. They take on the responsibility of fighting for our education system, our pupils and us teachers to ensure that we are getting the best that we can in schools and to push for improvements to be made within our industry. There's no way that we, as busy teachers, could dedicate as much time and energy to meeting politicians, canvassing opinions and campaigning on projects as the teaching unions do. We have the passion and the patience, but we also have full-time jobs that mean we can't prioritise it! The unions also have brilliant insights into the national and international picture, which we can sometimes forget about as our tunnel vision focuses on the local situation.

It probably comes as no surprise that there is one big tip I have for you in this chapter, and it's to join a teaching union. It doesn't matter which one; find the one that fits your role and maybe even has the best offer when it comes to signing up. I admittedly chose mine because of a special new-teacher offer of £1 for four terms. Your union will be a guide and a helping hand during your career, as well as a backstop and safety net. Like insurance, union membership is a bit pricey and you hope to never use it – but you never regret having it when you need it.

I debated whether to include this chapter in the book, but as it's a true reflection on my first year in school and I wanted to mention the importance of belonging to a union, I had to. Oh, and because of what happened the next day...

26 Ofsted

My phone rang on the table. I was tempted to ignore it, although I knew my friend wouldn't mind me checking who it was.

'Why is she calling me? Sorry, it's my deputy head – can I just answer this?'

I had headed into London with another teacher friend on the day of the strike. We'd visited the protests in the morning and were grabbing some lunch before heading to see a midweek West End matinee – a luxury for a teacher. My mind was still very much on my decision to strike, and I still felt immensely guilty, but I figured if I wasn't getting paid that day I needed to make the most of the time and take a bit of a break. Unfortunately, the break was about to get ruined.

'What's up?' my friend mouthed, as she read the fear on my face before I'd even got off the phone.

'The best way to ruin today. We've got the call. Ofsted are in tomorrow.' I sighed and felt a sense of looming doom. Today, of all days! This felt like karma. However, I was determined not to let it ruin lunch as I finished off another slice of my pizza.

'Do you still want to go and see the show?'

'Well, I've been told to go in because we need to prepare for tomorrow... but I'm on strike.'

I was stuck on what to do, but my indecision soon turned to determination; I was not going to let this get in the way. I was on strike, and if I wasn't going to get paid, I wouldn't be setting foot in the building. It wasn't the school I was mad at; it was Ofsted.

Hours later, and after nearly losing my voice singing along to 'We Will Rock You', my stubbornness was waning fast. I remembered what I'd thought in the run-up to the strike day: I was doing this for my pupils and their long-term benefit. Rational thought kicked in, and I realised that going in that evening to get ready for the inspection would be a benefit to those same children and to my school. I owed them that much. Mr Nice Guy had returned, and I was soon in the car to work.

I had never felt so unsettled as I walked into the building, but I was glad to be met by the familiar figure of the deputy head – and with a smile. She knew I'd been unsure and was grateful that I'd made it in, a decision that she wanted me to come to by myself. My mind clicked into work mode instantly, and that sense of teamwork was back at the forefront.

The evening was spent working with my year team to get things ready for the next day, ensuring my books were all marked according to policy, checking through plans for lessons I could potentially be observed in and swatting up on everything I could be asked about. It was like being on a uni all-nighter, cramming in revision before a big test. Luckily, unlike at university, I got home before midnight and managed to get some sleep before the big showdown (although not before ordering in what transpired to be my second pizza of the day).

Now, this chapter is going to be slightly different, because I am aware of two things:

1. Not everyone will be unlucky enough to have an Ofsted inspection during their first year of teaching.

2. Ofsted changes its frameworks regularly, meaning I can't give you the answers for what they will want to see and hear.

In fact, between my first inspection and my second one (four years later), there was a big difference, as by that time teachers no longer got individual gradings for Ofsted lesson observations. This was significant and seen as a positive by many teachers, although I was gutted that my one and only graded observation would forever be labelled as 'requires improvement'; it turned out that making Aztec masks wasn't deemed to be 'new learning', despite it being what we'd planned to do during our meetings the night before (I'm not still bitter about that one at all!).

What I can provide you with is some reassurance that the process isn't just focused on you, and that there is a point behind it all. The Office for Standards in Education, Children's Services and Skills (to give it its full title) is a non-ministerial department that states on the 'About Us' page of its website (in 2023) that it 'aims to improve lives by raising standards in education and children's social care'. It goes on, 'We inspect and regulate thousands of organisations and individuals providing education, training and care – from childminders to training providers, schools to local authorities – and we share what we find.' Essentially, it is Ofsted's job to check in with schools and ensure that the best is being done to provide education for pupils and to support schools in improving their offering and overall standards when there are identifiable ways in which to do so. You might think from the hearsay and hubbub caused whenever a school gets 'the call' that Ofsted's job is also to strike fear into teachers and anyone working in a place of education, but that isn't true. From experience, every time I have been part of an inspection, it's been a productive and positive experience, even if the school has been 'downgraded'.

There is an enormous amount of information on the Ofsted website and plenty of guidelines about how, where, when and why inspections happen, as well as what will occur. However, I want to bring up a few key moments that are pertinent to new teachers.

The call

Ofsted inspectors will call a school and speak to the headteacher (if possible) to make them aware that a visit is imminent, usually due the next day. This will trigger chaos ahead of the inspection, and you will likely find out it's coming when a member of the SLT knocks your door, looking like they've seen a ghost, inviting you to a whole-school meeting at lunchtime.

The briefing

On the morning of the inspection, the lead inspector (sometimes the only person carrying out the visit, depending on the size of the school and previous grading) will meet with as many staff as possible to introduce themselves and talk through the proceedings. It is a good opportunity to say hello and realise that they are human too, so attend if you can.

The inspection plan

Before anyone else from Ofsted steps into the school, the headteacher will formulate a plan with the lead inspector and decide on focus areas to steer the visit. These are usually based on the school's targets from its previous report or any areas that have changed dramatically since the last inspection. You should be informed of these by your SLT or in the briefing; if you don't know, ask!

The observations

During a visit, Ofsted inspectors will go into classrooms to gain first-hand experience of what learning is taking place. If observed, you will not be given a grading for this, but what is seen will feed into the overall verdict on the quality of education offered. You will likely get some feedback from an SLT member accompanying the inspector. You may not always get a warning about whether you will be observed, so it's best to be prepared.

The conversations

Depending on the lines of inquiry, you may be asked to speak with an inspector during their visit. I had to do so as a subject leader in my second inspection, and I discussed how we assessed pupil attainment and progress in science, as it was a target from the last inspection. Again, you should be told if you are due

Ofsted

to meet with an inspector and what the focus will be. One of the areas that could be chosen as a key focus is the school's provision for new teachers, and you would expect to be called up for that. Stay calm and remember that your conversation will only play a small part in the whole-school effort. You are not on trial, and no one is trying to trick you. Be honest, positive and friendly.

The wait

There are lots of different ways that the visit could go and end, determined by the type of inspection and outcome. Regardless, there will always be a wait while the inspector goes away and collates their report. Your headteacher should have a likely idea of the results, but they will usually keep this secret until the final stage.

The report

A few weeks after the visit, the official Ofsted report is released, containing details of the inspection as well as the all-important grading. This will be shared publicly on the Ofsted website and by the school.

***

While my first Ofsted experience didn't have the best outcome, it wasn't an experience that scarred me at all. I enjoyed seeing the school running at its best and seeing how, when the need arose, we could give our all. As teachers, we love a challenge, and this is a big one. Don't panic or worry; you will be brilliant. Go out there and be the best you can be.

Of course, there is one more option: some of my teacher friends play the system by leaving schools when an Ofsted visit is approaching and moving to schools that have just been inspected. No visit in 20 years is the best record I've heard of!

Top tips and tricks

1. Stay calm. It might sound silly, but panicking about Ofsted isn't the job of the teachers, because while we want to do our very best, we are just a few of the many people in the spotlight. All you need to do is be on top form, and you can do that easily.

2. Check in with your mentor as soon as you get the news. They are likely to be very busy over the next few hours, so grabbing them for advice and tips is something to do early on. They might have experienced inspections before and have some shining pearls of wisdom for you.

3. Take advice. Listen to your colleagues, especially those who are familiar with the process. They might be able to clue you in on what to prioritise and what to do to be ready. If you are part of a year team, you might decide on what you are going to do together.

4. Take a few minutes to revise your School Development Plan, whole-school targets and any school values or visions. Inspectors will often ask a cross section of people about these and expect to hear confident and consistent answers. Being a new teacher, you are more likely to be on that list.

5. Be open, and try your best. Whatever happens, all you can do is give the best you can on the day and learn from it. During my first inspection, I was friendly, open to interactions and determined to be my best. The resulting judgment hurt a little, but it gave me a new starting point and a new direction in which to develop myself.

27 Governors

You know when you have a question that burns away inside you, and you are just waiting for the right moment to ask it? Well, that was me. I'd made my decision. I'd got up and planned my strategy. How was I going to get over to her to ask?

I'd first met the woman on the morning of my job interview; she'd offered me a smile when I was at my most nervous. It had been promising to have a friendly face in the room, and it had definitely helped put my mind at ease. Interviews were stressful enough without having miserable or nonplussed faces looking back at you. Next, I'd seen her at the September Inset day. She had stood up to introduce herself to the staff, but it seemed most people were familiar with her already. Her next appearance was at our 'Meet the Teachers' evening, when she'd sat next to our headteacher, across the hall from me and my year team. Her main role that night was to greet the parents, mingle and then speak to everyone about our school budgets, which would benefit from support through the Parent–Teacher Association (PTA). In fact, she'd kept popping up – at subject-leader meetings, the Christmas fair, carol concerts, the end-of-term drinks and this afternoon at a special gathering in the hall to celebrate our Ofsted outcome. I decided it was time to make my move.

Meandering through various teachers and support staff and our office team (who were enjoying a rare and deserved hour away from phones and emails), I managed to grab her attention and say hello.

'James! How are you? How was your first Ofsted?'

I didn't want to make her aware that I'd managed to mess up my part of the inspection completely – and if she already knew, she was being kind enough to spare my embarrassment by not confronting me with it.

'Yeah, it was all right. Not the most enjoyable experience in the world, but at least we know it'll be a while until the next one.' We both laughed with relief. I decided this was the moment to ask, although I could feel the redness ready to hit my face at any moment.

'I wanted to come over and see if I could ask you a quick question.'

She nodded her approval.

'Umm… well, I know that you are the chair of governors, but what is it that you and the governors actually do?'

I felt the red starting to rise, realising just how rudely that could have come across. Luckily, my question was met with laughter.

'Ha! You aren't the first person to ask me that, and you won't be the last.'

I remember the moment I braved this question because of just how embarrassed I was to ask it. Here was someone who was clearly involved in our school in a substantial capacity, but I didn't really understand what that role was. I could have searched for an answer online, but I thought it better to ask directly to find out what the governors did in our school specifically. I knew that they must wield some sort of power within the place, since I'd had two governors on my interview panel, but I wanted to understand it a bit more. The irony was that after having the conversation and learning what a governor does, I ended up becoming one myself. I even got asked the same question months later and replied with the same response I'd received.

The remit of the governing body is the same in all schools – driving the school's strategic overview and vision, being responsible for the financial business of the school, holding leaders to account to ensure efficiency and effectiveness and monitoring the performance of pupils and staff. The DfE says in its 2020 'Governance handbook' that governors must be 'ambitious for all children and young people and infused with a passion for education and a commitment to continuous school improvement that enables the best possible outcomes.' On the ground, these figures are responsible for everything – decisions on how to spend the school's funds to refurbish and develop the school site, monitoring and analysis of the school's performance data, challenging the headteacher and school staff about the effectiveness and value of the school, signing off on new projects, overseeing the balancing of the books and making sure that the school can keep running and moving in the right direction. Quite a big task for a group of volunteers!

Each school's governing body will look different, depending on the size and type of the school. For example, academy trusts might have a small local governing body for each school and an executive governing body or board overseeing all the schools in the trust. The school I worked in had 15 of us governors leading the way, which was on the larger end of the scale. The group will usually have smaller committee groups as part of it too; these will meet regularly to look in depth at a facet of school life and prepare reports to feed back to the full governing body. I used to sit on the curriculum committee (reviewing what was taught and the pupils' performance), the personnel committee (looking at the workforce and trying to ensure we had a happy and effective group of staff) and the finance committee (monitoring the money and signing off on expenditure with a view to ensuring the best value). There are also groups and governors focused on pay, premises, admissions, pupils, SEND and most other areas of school life.

While it might sound quite scary, and you may feel uncomfortable with a bunch of voluntary non-teachers running the school, this arrangement does have significant benefits. It takes some monumental decisions away from us teachers and our SLTs, it allows staff to focus on the operational day-to-day parts of their roles and it means that decisions are informed by the varied experiences of the people making up the governing body. As the National Governance Association (2023) says on its website as part of its eight elements of effective governance, it is important to have 'the right people around the table' with an 'understanding [of] the role and responsibilities', who know the school and are 'committed to asking challenging questions'. Governors must have the school's best interests at heart, and their hearts must be in the right place. Rest assured, in the vast majority of schools they will be a joy to work with and will be helping your practice, your children and your school to shine in the best light they can.

There's one of the Teachers' Standards that you can primarily apply when working alongside governors.

Standard		Evidence
8	Professional behaviours	Working alongside your school's governors will mean playing your part in developing the school, its vision and its ethos as a member of the whole-school community. Any examples of relevant projects, meetings or work could be used as strong evidence.

Top tips and tricks

1. Find out who they are. Legally, your school's website must contain a list of governors in your school and the committees that they are a part of.

2. Introduce yourself. You will more than likely have met a governor or two at your job interview, but some schools have many more. Take the chance to say hello when they are in and around the school.

3. Discover the governors' roles. Most governors will be responsible for a specific area of school life or a subject; you might end up frequently working alongside a certain one. Again, this information should be on the school website, but if it isn't, you can ask for it.

4. Remember that they aren't teachers. You will have parent governors and community governors who won't have any experience or knowledge

of a classroom. If you are working with them, be confident in sharing your insight as a teacher, because it may be very valuable.

5. Consider becoming a governor. If one of your school's staff governors steps down, it is a good role for you to think about applying for. You will have to be elected by your colleagues, but for a few hours of volunteering a term you'll get a fascinating insight into how the school works and a better understanding of why things happen as they do. If you want to further your education career into leadership one day, this is an amazing early opportunity to support that goal.

28 Bank holidays

I have always wondered why weeks start on a Monday. Yes, I was one of those 'why children' at school – but there had to be someone or something behind that convention. The reason this question had crept back into my consciousness was that the fact I wasn't starting the working week on a Monday, thanks to a bank holiday, was causing me to mess everything up.

Nothing had gone wrong getting into school (in fact, I'd suffered a 6.00 am alarm on the bank holiday to make sure I didn't forget to switch the alarm back on, because I didn't need that extra anxiety), but it wasn't long after I'd got into the classroom that I started tripping up. I'd written 'Monday' on the whiteboard before remembering it was a Tuesday, and I'd realised that

I wouldn't get the Monday assembly time I'd been counting on to get some last-minute paperwork finished. Pretty minor things, I know, but it didn't stop there.

9.00 am rolled around, and my class were their sparky selves, which is always my preferred classroom culture. It turned out that three-day weekends were just as revitalising for children as they were for adults! Well, it was that and the fact I'd put Monday's visual timetable on the board, so my poor pupils thought I'd been nice enough to negotiate moving their missed computing and PE lessons to Tuesday. The news that their afternoon would actually be taken up by English and science wasn't received with such enthusiasm. Hey, we all have a 'whoops moment' every now and then, don't we?

By break time, I was still in the wrong time zone… or day zone… I wrote the wrong date in a child's book, and caused outrage when I inadvertently short-changed the class with only two days instead of three to do their homework (luckily, this was fixed before the parents found out). I was glad to find I wasn't the only one in the staffroom suffering with it all, and I laughed along with other teachers' stories over my break time cuppa – until we realised it was five minutes after break and no whistle had been blown. I experienced a horrible rush of guilt and panic as I once again realised it was Tuesday and that my break duty jacket and whistle were still hanging up.

By the afternoon, I had pretty much got a grasp on reality again and, just like every New Year, I was eventually on board with remembering the right date. My class were brilliant, as always, at finding the funny side of it all, and they were pleased to get an extra five minutes on the playground in the afternoon to make up for my timetable faux pas in the morning.

The end of the day finally came around. Without much marking to do, I decided to get out early and work from home for a couple of hours. I'd be more productive powering through my planning and data-crunching on the sofa with some music. I grabbed my bag and coat and headed out, saying goodbye to my head and deputy head as I reached the office. Their faces were confused as they questioned me, their diaries and hot drinks in hand.

'James, where are you going? It's Tuesday. Staff meeting? I think this explains where you were at break time too...'

Any time off, as I've discussed in the book so far, is always well received, but bank holidays are like little gifts for teachers and glimpses into the four-day weeks that are starting to be explored by business sectors around the world. Hundreds of big companies around the world have been trialling the format since the organisation 4 Day Week Global paved the way with a pioneering study. The research found that working one day less each week made employees feel less burned out, gave them more time for exercise and reduced the number of people suffering from sleep problems. All in all, it sounds pretty positive. Now, we obviously can't move to a full four-day-week structure in schools without resigning ourselves to (a quick bit of maths...) three weeks of holiday every year – but we can make the most of these little power-ups when they do come around. Personally, my approach to bank holidays is making the most of both the extra day off and the shortened week that follows.

While it's common for teachers to assign some of their half terms and holidays to work, I treat my bank holidays as if they are sacred; I do not and will not do anything related to school on those days. Why? Well, if you were working in any other job and you had the day off, would you be expected to sit at home focusing on what should have been? No! Thinking back to my earlier chapter about the work–life balance, I consider this a day to put myself first. I see bank holidays as days for adventures, road trips, experiences and 'me time'. If you have children at home too, it might be slightly different – a family day out or a day to mix things up at home. The key thing is to enjoy the time you've been given and do whatever you need to do to reap the benefits of it.

When it comes to the remaining four days of the week, I perceive them as 'power weeks' when I can focus on getting more done, as I only need to split my energy between four days. Often, these will be the weeks when I will try and tackle a display, write an assembly or finish off a project that's been sitting on my 'to do' list for a little while. Anything that could benefit from additional enthusiasm and productivity is worth scheduling in for these weeks, as you can attack them with a boost and often get satisfaction and gratification from completing them. From experience, there will be some schools out there where this can be tough as Monday's tasks are not cancelled or rescheduled, and some teachers might darken your door with the classic pessimism of 'having four days to do five days' worth of work is just an inconvenience'. If this is the case, chat with your mentor or raise it with your year team; is there something that can be moved or eliminated that would allow staff to get the full benefit of a bank holiday without the added pressure of doing the same amount of work in less time?

Wellbeing is rightly a big focus in schools, and it should be a top priority for new teachers, especially as you get used to the pace and rigour of the teaching role. Being successful as a teacher involves a lot of hard work, but just as importantly it is about knowing how to work smart, and when not to work at all. There is no shame in taking a breather and letting yourself catch up with the pace before getting back on the treadmill. If anything, I respect those who do this even more!

While bank holidays aren't going to provide you with evidence for the Teachers' Standards, there are two 'side effects' that could be useful to consider.

Standard		Evidence
4	Classroom practice	A shortened week may require some clever adaptation of your planning, especially if you are using schemes or programmes. Demonstrating your ability to devise a changed plan that still leads to success against objectives is excellent proof that you are reaching Teachers' Standard 4.
P2	Personal and professional conduct	A key component of the Part Two standards is maintaining your own attendance and punctuality – something that can be affected if you aren't sure which day it is! Being on top of your diary and ensuring you turn up to meetings scheduled for a different day is a way of showing your commitment to your own professionalism.

Top tips and tricks

1. Get the bank holidays in your diary early. You'll be surprised how much the extra day off can have a knock-on effect!

2. Get yourself ready for Tuesday morning. Make sure your Friday afternoon is spent preparing for the correct day, as it helps you make the most of an easy start to your shortened week.

3. Keep an eye on meetings moving to another day on a bank holiday week. Check your emails and ask around to avoid any embarrassing absences.

4. Switch off on the day. It may be a weekday, but it shouldn't be a work day! Take the day to relax, and avoid any emails or phone calls from work.

5. Give the four remaining days your all. I used to appreciate the shorter weeks, as I could split my energy across four days instead of five. I tended to find that they were the most productive weeks I had.

29 Wet playtimes

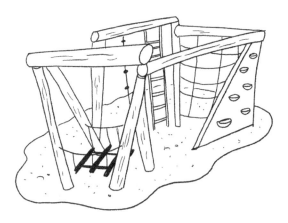

We all groaned as the bell rang for yet another wet play. It was nearly Thursday lunchtime, and none of us wanted to be stuck inside again. There'd been brilliant sunshine to start the week, but after a dry Monday morning, clouds stubbornly set about raining on our parade… well, playground.

'Sorry, everyone. Wet play again. Don't worry though – it means you can finish watching Despicable Me!' There was a half-hearted cheer as my class searched for some positive in the situation. I did feel for them. They needed to stretch their legs, get some fresh air and enjoy a bit of freedom. Looking at the forecast, it seemed unlikely that they'd be getting that for the rest of the week (but I didn't want to break that news just yet).

After eating my lunch and heading back to get things ready for the afternoon, I found my kids sitting enthralled by the movie, and I was proud of them for proving how much I'm able to trust them. They are a great bunch, and that helps during times like these, let me tell you. With five minutes to go, I noticed there were three chairs still empty, but most had made it back from eating in the hall. The clock ticked past 1.15 pm, and while everyone was converting the room back out of 'cinema mode', those three seats remained unclaimed. It was strange because Amir, Bailey and Zain are usually back in pretty quickly. I asked my TA if she could check with the office to see if they'd gone for a magic paper towel or ice pack, but she came back with no children and a worried look on her face. Where on Earth were they?

Ten minutes later, the deputy head had come down to ask if I'd found the trio. I shook my head, and she assured me that she'd take over the search. Mild panic was starting to set in by this point – it always does when there's a need to involve the SLT. How had I managed to lose three children in a building on my lunch break? Why had none of the other children seen them? Were they playing a prank on me? I knew I'd pulled a great April Fool's Day joke on them recently, maybe this was their revenge. But I didn't want to be explaining that to my headteacher. My heart wasn't really in the lesson I was delivering as I nervously watched people popping their head around our door and heard the names of the three missing children being called from the corridors. The passing minutes crept up, 1.30 pm became 2.00 pm and my heart rate kept rising, until a knock on the door interrupted me mid-sentence. In walked the deputy, followed by three drenched children looking sheepish with a little hint of pride.

'They decided to ignore the fact it was wet play and make a break for it. I found them on the climbing frame on the playground.'

The class fizzed with murmurs and disbelief as the boys squelched to their seats. I was disappointed that the boys had been so irresponsible, but I won't lie: I was somewhat impressed that they'd managed to duck out of the hall and get around the school to the climbing frame without being seen, and then hide inside it for nearly an hour. It wouldn't have been professional to give them credit for their ingenuity at that moment, but I knew the words 'creative', 'cunning' and 'adaptable' would be featuring in their end-of-year reports.

'Come and sit down, boys. You'll have to hope your clothes dry out quickly, so you aren't uncomfortable and cold.'

A sigh of relief came. What a drama! I suppose it was something to spice up the mundanity of what had become 'wet play week'.

I challenge you to find me a single person who genuinely likes wet playtime. Didn't think so! Staff hate having the children inside and in the way, students hate being cooped up and nobody benefits from the lack of fresh air. It's a necessary evil and inconvenience, but there are ways to minimise the impact that it has on learning.

As teachers, we know from what we see daily that our children benefit from being active at break times, so it doesn't surprise me that when pupils have been restricted inside four walls their ability to focus is limited. The EEF asserts, based on its moderate evidence, that physical activity has an impact on pupils and their education. Exercise gets the heart pumping and the blood flowing to the brain more rapidly. What's the effect of that? Better thinking. A study in 2007, by Winter et al., found that when a group of children was learning new vocabulary, they were 20 percent faster at doing so after exercise compared to beforehand. When our pupils don't get the chance to get up and move around, it can be harder for them to process what they are learning, and this can have knock-on consequences for their mood and behaviour. My way to tackle this has always been to take my class for a walk around the school, sneak five minutes in the hall to get moving or use dance routines and movement-break videos on YouTube. Whatever you do, raising energy levels physically will also help to raise them mentally.

Aside from affecting learning, wet play can have an impact on your pupils' emotions (as well as yours and your colleagues'). You know that glum feeling you get when you open the curtains only to be faced with grey clouds and torrential rain? Well, it can be a substantial downer on how we feel and a total killer of any work ethic you have mustered up that day. My remedy? Transform your classroom into an environment that's a bit sunnier and brighter. Play upbeat music to drown out the rain hitting the windows, open the vents to get some fresh air into the room and make sure the classroom is nice and light. Not only that, but allow yourself to smile more with your children, because keeping them smiling and feeling positive will encourage them to stay calmer. Ultimately, create some sunshine inside your classroom to keep the clouds at bay.

Oh, and on the topic of behaviour, be prepared that you might have to be stronger than usual with your behaviour management to keep on top of things. There is a chapter coming up to help you with that.

There's no wet play standard in the Teachers' Standards, but wet play can link to a couple of areas.

Standard		Evidence
1	High expectations	High expectations aren't just needed in lessons; challenging your pupils to be independently self-organised and motivated to get ready for their afternoon lessons on time is a good skill and habit for later life.
7	Managing behaviour	'Feral' may be a strong word, but it isn't far off how a class can be after a day cooped up inside. Strong behaviour-management skills and strategies may be needed to keep them focused on learning in the afternoon, and this is a chance to reflect on your own practice, all feeding into Teachers' Standard 7.

Top tips and tricks

1. Check your school's policy or routine. Most schools will have a procedure for wet play that says who will be based where and what will happen. This is the perfect place to start and should be a document that you familiarise yourself with early on. Also, consider the safeguarding guidance too – letting children loose on YouTube may not be an appropriate decision!

2. Set a routine. Minimise any wasted learning time by telling your class what you want them to do at the end of wet play so that they are ready for the next lesson. After a few practices, they should be ready and raring to go before the bell.

Wet playtimes

3. Consider your transitions. On days when the pupils haven't been out to stretch their legs, make sure to get a brain break between each lesson and go for something which gets them up and moving.

4. Open some windows. Rain shouldn't stop you opening a window or two. It's vital to keep fresh air circulating around the classroom for everyone's health, focus and attention.

5. Empower through responsibility. Grant some of your class jobs during wet playtimes. You could have tidy-up monitors, board-game allocators or, as I had, 'multimedia minions' to sort out the movie or TV programme that we'd be watching in the 'classroom cinema'. It's a super chance to give an occasional responsibility to someone who would benefit from it.

30 The summer fair

Last Friday was one of the rare occasions when I joined in with the grumbles from my colleagues as our head made his announcement in the weekly briefing.

'Remember, it's the summer fair a week on Sunday. The sign-up sheet is going to be in the staffroom from Monday, so make sure you add your name to one of the time slots. We expect you all to come in and help, and while I respect that it's your weekend, I am sure you can give the school an hour of your time.'

With the year coming to a close, I was knee deep in test papers, frantically writing reports and focusing on my looming ECT assessment. The last thing I wanted to do on a Sunday afternoon was feign a smile and stand behind the bottle tombola for an hour while the grandma of a Year 2 pupil complained that her £10 worth of tickets only won her a bottle of tomato ketchup. Unfortunately, it seemed like the emotional-blackmail card was being used; there's a limited number of times that we allow 'for the good of the children' to be used as a rationale at our school when it comes to losing evenings and weekends. As it was, by Thursday, I realised that the head was right, and I went to the staffroom to put my name down for a slot.

Walking into the room, I saw that none of my colleagues had followed the rules we'd been given ('Three people per time slot, and make sure nothing is left empty, please').

Looking down the list, six people had decided to take the earliest stint on the bottle tombola, cramming their names into the box made for three. The list of names to sell raffle tickets and programmes at the front gate was just as full. Again, some clever people had raced into the earliest time slot, freeing up the rest of the day. It seemed like everyone had beaten me to it, so obviously my help wasn't needed!

'Ah, well done for signing up, although you've left it a bit late.' The voice of our deputy head interrupted my thoughts of slowly walking away and hoping no-one would notice I was missing from the rota. 'But don't worry; this one has plenty of spaces. It always seems to!'

I feigned a smile – good practice for the weekend – but that disappeared immediately as I saw what stall I'd be on. It was bad enough losing an hour of a sunny weekend when I had a mountain of work to do, but I was not looking forward to spending 1.00–2.00 pm that Sunday in the stocks. 'Sponge the teacher'… it should be a crime.

Funnily enough, despite my uncharacteristic moodiness the week prior, the fair was a success, and I was pleased to be involved. It was a beautifully hot day, and I didn't mind the refreshing chill from the occasional accurately thrown sponge (we won't mention the fact that I moved the throwing line a couple of metres further back after the deputy finished her shift). Besides, it was brilliant seeing people coming together for some fun and to support the local school.

Attending the fair gave me a chance to meet the extended families and friends of my pupils (and hear what stories the children had relayed to those at home) and get a glimpse into their lives – although sometimes I wished I'd had the chance earlier, as it would have helped me understand the child a bit better! There was also the opportunity to get a better understanding of the local community I was in. People from all around ventured in to enjoy something from the barbecue, take their kids on the bouncy castle or try their luck with the bottle tombola. Seeing the community that exists beyond the front gates of the school you work in gives you a greater insight into how the children operate and what matters to them, while also allowing you to preview the recruits from upcoming year groups and realise which of the younger siblings of your current class you might want to avoid in years to come!

Most importantly though, events like these are essential for schools and their funding. Finances have been a difficulty for most public and state schools for a long time, and whenever you are picking up this book and reading this chapter, I doubt it will have changed. Events run by your school's PTA – which will likely have a quirky name, as they all tend to nowadays – are a vital source of additional funding that can help bring an extra sparkle to your job. I've seen fundraising targets for new reading books, playground equipment, learning resources, a class tablet and an end-of-year trip. Each school and demographic is different; I've worked in schools that will make £20,000 in an afternoon and others that will make £200. The truth is that money determines the impact that schools can have on their pupils and their education offering, so any way of bringing in some extra cash to balance the books and provide something exciting or special is worth it.

You might have heard horror stories of PTA parents being elitist dictators or being roped in because no one else would take on the job, but I can reassure you that they all mean well and want to contribute their time and efforts to help their child's school be at its best. You might get the occasional one thinking that being chair of the committee means their child gets special privileges, but more often than not they all just want what is best for their child. We all have a lot more in common than we sometimes realise.

Turning up for the fair might be an inconvenience if it's awkwardly timed, but it can be another source of evidence for the Teachers' Standards.

Standard		Evidence
8	Professional behaviours	This is another opportunity to get involved with the school community and a good example of how you contribute to the wider school (if you don't have some evidence already by this point). I know an ECT who photocopied the sign-up sheet and highlighted their name for proof!

Top tips and tricks

1. Check what the protocol is. Each school manages its fairs and events differently, so find out what is expected of you beforehand.

2. Find someone to volunteer with. If you are expected to give up some of your evening or weekend to attend an event, try partnering with a work friend or colleague who will help the time go quickly. Having a laugh makes these moments a lot more fun!

3. Volunteer early. Ask if there will be a sign-up sheet and when it will go up; you don't want to be left with the last choice.

4. If you can't go, be honest and let your headteacher know. I've missed a school event because of a big family birthday party, and a friend of mine skipped one because of a wedding. It happens, but it's better to say something instead of signing up and not turning up.

5. Check in with your class. Sometimes your class might be responsible for an element of an event. If this is the case, take a couple of minutes to visit them and show your support. It means a lot to the parents and children volunteering when we appreciate their time and effort.

31 Behaviour

They say that no two days in a classroom are the same. That, to me, is an understatement.

Now that I was in the final half term of my first year, and – being a reflective practitioner and all that – I had spent time looking back over the year that had been, I'd realised that while the timetables had stayed similar, the topics had stuck around for a while and the pupils on the register had remained the same, every day had been full of unpredictability. But that was one of the reasons I loved the job – even after one of the most horrendous days I'd ever had when it came to behaviour. I felt proud with how I managed it though.

Wednesdays hadn't been easy that year; English, maths and spelling made for an intensive morning, and were followed up by history, guided reading and assembly in the afternoon. It wasn't the most riveting of days for my pupils, and while I always tried my best to add in some fun and engagement, it was never going to match a PE or science day. That particular day's odds were stacked even further out of my favour by a reading test in English, assembly being cancelled and the weather providing an impromptu day-long downpour. We'd been learning about rainforests, so 'hot' and 'humid' were very much part of our class vocabulary at that moment – I just didn't want to experience them in my classroom.

The day started normally – whatever that meant – and by 10.30 am, the test was over. An hour of silent working had taken it out of everyone, so a quick brain break led into maths, and by 11.15 am, things were looking good. A false sense of security was creeping in. Fool.

One of my colleagues often used an analogy about behaviour and the ability to self-regulate, which likened children to cans of fizzy drink: when things went wrong and they got overstimulated, it was like shaking the can and making the pressure build up inside. When a child was able to self-regulate, they let their can rest and allowed the pressure to reduce. However, sometimes, it continued to build until they needed to open the ring pull and let it escape. That was what happened just before lunch.

'F*** off!'

It wasn't the first time I'd heard a child swear in class (and it wouldn't be the last). Some children were shocked, and they swivelled to work out who the word had come from. Others snickered to themselves or to the friend next to them. I noticed two of my more 'behaviourally challenged' pupils catch eyes across the room, a knowing signal that this could be their chance to join the fray. My quick-but-firm 'Don't!' stopped them in their tracks as they went to open their mouths. I was shocked by the outburst, but I'd entered the strange state that teachers slip into when they sense something is about to happen: a state of adrenaline, reflexive reactions and assertiveness. I turned to look at the child whose voice I recognised and prepared to give him the warning he deserved. It was at that moment the chair flew past my face. The ring pull was open.

Going back to the fizzy-drink-can analogy, many of us know what happens when a shaken drink is opened – there's a relentless mess as the pressure is released and the drink empties everywhere. When I think about it now, that was how the situation looked in the moment. The swearing and chair-throwing was followed by Dino picking up his partner's ruler and snapping it in half. I'd started making my way over to intervene, because my biggest worry was somebody getting hurt (although luckily the chair had cleared everyone that it flew over). As I reached Dino and used an open hand to carefully manoeuvre him towards the classroom door, a rubber was thrown at the window, the table leg was kicked, a punch was thrown my way to stop me removing him from the situation and a final swear word was thrown in for good measure. My TA was brilliant in closing the door behind me, as I continued to steer Dino towards a safe space, and then calming down the class before getting them to carry on looking at words ending in '-ence'.

I'd never seen such a monumental reaction before, and I was surprised it had come from Dino, who is usually one of the happiest boys in the class. I was shaking from adrenaline as I sat beside the headteacher, working out what had caused the commotion. Dino finally conceded the answer once he'd calmed down: his table partner, Tiana, had been tapping her pen on the table, and he'd asked her to stop. When she didn't and the pen hit his hand, he couldn't control it.

No two days are the same in the classroom. I didn't think I'd end up seeing a flying chair that year, but when the time came, I dealt with it and nobody got hurt. Sure, I had paperwork, a parent call and an entry in the safeguarding system to do, but the day remained a win in my book.

Behaviour is the single most discussed element of our job when I work with trainee or new teachers. It is the thing that worries us (and sometimes scares us) the most. Why? I have always wondered if it's our reluctance to believe that we could manage situations like the one with Dino or if it's the fear of being outnumbered thirty to one! My answer for how to deal with behaviour is that it is a mix of your experience, your own strategies and your knowledge of the pupils. When the time comes, your instinct and reflexes kick in much more quickly than you expect.

The best way to feel prepared is to read and observe the different strategies and systems that teachers use to promote positive behaviour and to signpost the wrong choices of behaviour, to support children in understanding where things have gone wrong. I am a firm believer that behaviour is about choices, and I never tell a child that they are naughty or bad, although I admittedly have to bite my tongue sometimes. If a child often finds it challenging to make the right decision, help them by making clear what choices they have and giving positive praise when they do the correct thing. If I'd given Dino the choice to throw the chair and lose his lunchtime or not throw the chair and take some time out of the classroom to calm down instead, I know he would have selected the latter.

I believe it's also important to separate 'behaviour' from 'behaviour for learning'. These two often get combined, but they come from different places. Behaviour is about ensuring children act in a way that aligns with positive values, morals and attitudes, choosing right over wrong. Behaviour for learning is all about displaying the attributes of a good learner and choosing to listen, focus, get involved and try your best. I have worked with pupils who have brilliant behaviour for learning but struggle with their overall behaviour because of their social skills and inability to make an instinctive and quick decision in certain situations.

There is no 'one size fits all' solution, and while I wish I had the magic key to unlocking perfect behaviour, nobody does. All I can do is offer you my experiences and my tips. However, there is an easy solution for where it comes in the Teachers' Standards.

Standard		Evidence
7	Managing behaviour	Unsurprisingly, Teachers' Standard 7 is where evidence of behaviour management is most useful – both developing and successful. Extracts from observation feedback, reflections from observing your colleagues, a record of strategies you've used (with their impacts) or notes from CPD sessions about behaviour management can all demonstrate your journey to better practice.

Top tips and tricks

1. Start with the behaviour policy. It may not be your preferred style or strategy, but you should work from the whole-school policy when it comes to rewards and sanctions. It provides you with a structure, confidence that you are following the same rules as others and reassurance that you'll get support from the rest of your school community.

2. Try different strategies. Be open to new approaches, especially if you see something you think could work with your class. Remember, the ways to get the best behaviour for learning in your classroom specifically will usually come from you and your knowledge of the children.

3. Use your colleagues as a resource. Take an active look at what other teachers are doing in their classrooms to refresh your ideas, and ask for advice from your mentor, year team, SLT members and other colleagues. Behaviour is a school-wide focus, so supporting adults might have techniques that are even more successful than the teachers; leave no stone unturned!

4. Combine consistency with flexibility. Successful behaviour management comes from having clear boundaries and guidelines that are enforced regularly – but we work with children, not robots. Take time to reflect on why a child is behaving in a certain way and, if necessary, adapt your

behavioural system to allow them to reach your expectation. If a child's behaviour changes, that's something to monitor carefully for safeguarding concerns.

5. Remember it isn't personal. When the behaviour in your classroom isn't up to your standard, it can feel like it's a personal and purposeful choice made by your pupils. Most of the time, this is not the case. Try to explore why pupils are making their choices before blaming yourself and your practice.

32 Complaints

'Can you pop down to my office when the kids have gone home, please?'

These are words that strike fear into anyone's heart – and that was their effect on me when my headteacher swung by my classroom one afternoon. What could it be about? Was Ofsted coming? What had I forgotten to do? Ahh… I hated having to wait for a meeting with no idea of what it was about. I was distracted for the rest of the art lesson and was more keen than normal to get the children out at the end of the day.

After the last child left my room, I went down to the office to find out what was going on.

'OK, I'm sorry to have kept you waiting on this, but I wanted to leave it until the end of the day. Something happened yesterday with Ani at lunchtime, and you dealt with it afterwards, yes?'

I nodded.

'What happened?'

I spent a few moments thinking back carefully and then recounted how Ani had come back in from lunchtime upset. I'd asked what was wrong, and she'd told me that two girls from the class had been unkind to her. After that, I spoke to the two pupils in question and quizzed them on what had happened. Putting the two stories together gave me the bigger picture, and with the help of one of the adults on the playground I realised that Ani had been calling the two pupils unkind names before they retaliated. I wanted to get things sorted and get back to learning, so I had all three girls come out to listen to my verdict. When they all agreed on the truth, they all apologised, and I reminded them of our values, including kindness.

My headteacher listened carefully, legs folded, hand on chin, stoic – he'd have made a good detective. Once I finished the story, he came to his own verdict.

'I thought that was how it would have happened. Unfortunately, I had a couple of emails from parents this morning – one asking why you'd wasted twenty minutes of the lesson speaking with children out in the corridor (their words, not mine) and one from Ani's mum.'

He spun his computer round, and I scanned through the email.

'Disappointed'… 'didn't listen to my daughter'… 'blaming her for something she didn't do'… 'allowing them to bully her'… 'unprofessional'… 'not supporting my child'… 'upset and doesn't want to come to school'… 'not the first time'… 'wish for this to be dealt with by someone else so it can be dealt with properly'.

The words stung as I read them all. Not only had I 'wasted' my lesson time trying to deal with the issue, but it had all been for nothing. My guess was that Ani had shared stories about her day at home, and either she'd left out some key details or her mum had decided not to listen properly.

'Look, I believe what you're saying, but could you ring Mum and discuss it with her?'

I honestly couldn't think of anything worse than picking up the phone to call a disappointed and disgruntled parent, who less than 12 hours before had essentially been calling me names.

━━━━━━━━━━━━━━━━━━━━━━━━━━━━━━━━

My story, while true, doesn't reflect how devastated and upset I was about getting a complaint from a parent. Many of us put everything into our jobs and care a great deal about what we do. Unfortunately, that fact means that when someone feels the need to be negative about what we have done, it can really hurt. In fact, teachers are notorious for being perfectionistic, overly self-critical and fixated on their own weaknesses; we don't really need other people doing that for us!

Complaints are commonplace in teaching because of what we do: working with children, most of whom have parents and guardians who want the best for them and will fight to the death for them, all while believing them to be above anyone else. If you had your own child and they came to you crying at the end of the school day, I'm sure you'd be feeling the same way. We are all human, after all. But it means that we teachers often come under scrutiny for how we've managed a situation, for how something has been taught, for how something has been said or even for things that haven't been said or done. It's almost impossible to please everyone all the time, so this is to be expected. The reason I am telling you this is because it means you shouldn't always panic when the email alert sounds or a member of your SLT tells you that they've heard from a parent or guardian. Often, the truth will prevail.

Another truth to share with you is that most complaints, especially those lodged over email, come across much worse than they are meant. Not being able to have a conversation or see the expressions of the person making the grievance means it's much more difficult to gauge the situation. I've had emails from parents in the past that have sounded fiery, but when I've spoken to them on the phone they've been a lot more reasonable and amicable. You must also watch out for late evening emails. I have had some horrible ones, but I quickly learned that those emails were often sent by parents who had been dealing with long days, traffic-filled commutes and then a couple of glasses of something to take the edge off.

Of course, there are some schools and areas that may be more challenging, and parents may choose to confront you at school instead of sending an email. I've had this happen once before, and I was inwardly terrified as an aggressive parent shouted me down on the playground. Luckily, my colleagues were around, and we were able to move on and defuse the situation quickly. It's rare, but it can happen.

When all is said and done, I don't want you to dwell on the negatives that are misinformed or misguided, but you should heed any little bits of guidance and reflections that are well informed and well mannered. Acting on feedback is a part of Teachers' Standard 8 and is an essential part of success in any career. The important message here is remembering that complaints are different to feedback, especially if they only cover half of the story.

It's always good to find a positive in a negative, like when you can use complaints to help you evidence the Teachers' Standards!

Standard		Evidence
1	High expectations	We all make mistakes, and taking the opportunity to model honesty, respect and forgiveness around these is important in teaching your pupils the attitudes and values covered in Teachers' Standard 1.
8	Professional behaviours	Communicating with parents is a big part of Teachers' Standard 8, as it shows you are working alongside people in the wider school community. Records of meetings or email correspondence around a complaint, especially one that finds a solution, are good evidence for this.

Top tips and tricks

1. Be upfront and communicate clearly. It's important to face up to any complaints and find solutions. When talking with parents, guardians or colleagues, speak calmly and clearly to help reach an outcome sooner. Phone calls or face-to-face conversations can be better than emails, which can be misunderstood.

2. Work with your mentor and colleagues. If you get a complaint from a parent or guardian, you can always ask for advice. Read the complaint through with

your mentor first to help you start thinking of a plan of action.

3. It's OK to be sad and then move on. Complaints can be upsetting, especially as we put our hearts and souls into the job. It's totally fine to be emotional about the situation, but when it is sorted, make sure not to dwell on it.

4. Reflect. Linking to the previous point, learn from your mistakes and any complaints by thinking about what you can do better next time. Once you have thought about what you can take away from the situation, leave it behind you.

5. Don't take it out on the child. This may seem a little controversial, but we have all done it: a child has a parent or guardian who likes to moan about every little thing, and our reaction is to stop giving the child as much as we already do. The child has often done nothing wrong in this situation, so while it can be hard to stay civil with them after you've had your head bitten off, try your best.

33 Sports day

Away from the classroom, I love watching sport and have seen pretty much every Olympic Games that I have been alive for (as well as being lucky enough to work at a few of them). Why do I love them so much? It's the drama, the emotion, the celebration of the best on the world's biggest stage. I didn't realise that a primary school sports day could bring two out of the three.

The morning kicked off with every student and staff member sardining themselves into the hall. Our PE lead stood at the front, children sitting on her toes, with the projector showing the day's plan of action. It felt more like a battle briefing as she showed us where each of the 16 stations would be on the playground and field, before explaining the objective of each. The scoring system reminded me of the Eurovision Song Contest; it was just as complex and confusing, but it would get us to a winning house. Not a minute too soon, we all filed out of the hall and on to the playground. The sun was blazing hot (not too surprising on a July day) and there was equipment as far as the eye could see: beanbags, hoops, balls of different shapes and sizes, bibs, bands, goals, cones and things I had only seen shoved down the back of the PE cupboard until now. It was all quite exciting.

It didn't take long for the drama to start. We'd got through three of the rotations, and things were going well as a fourth bunch came to me for their turn at the beanbag toss. The whistle blew, and we were off. We'd split the children into smaller teams within their houses and across the year groups. It was lovely to see the oldest and youngest pupils working well together. There was plenty of cheering and encouragement, super fair play and some brilliant accuracy too. However, I looked across and saw Samira, a girl from Year 6, looking out of sorts. She wasn't her normal chatty self; her eyes weren't focusing and she looked confused. I watched as she went to throw her next beanbag and started slumping to the ground. I ran towards her. Two of her friends went to the first-aid table to summon help, and I sat with her, trying to keep her cool, using my hat as shade for her face. The rest of her team realised what was going on and started panicking. There were tears, screams and some very keen Year 3 pupils trying to see what was going on. Luckily, she recovered quite quickly and spent the rest of the morning watching from under the first-aid tent, cheering on her house. The cause? Samira and her family were observing Ramadan, and this was her first year of attempting fasting. With the early summer sunrise – six hours before her collapse – and her abstinence from drinking and eating, the heat got too much.

The morning finished with a closely fought battle between the houses, and after we'd crowned a winner, it was on to lunch and an afternoon of races with the parents coming along to spectate from the sidelines.

I promised emotions, and the afternoon was full of them: pride as my class set out on sprint, long-distance, egg-and-spoon and sack races, joy when we achieved a gold-medal sticker and reassurance when someone was disappointed with their performance. The one that got me was the final sprint race, in which one of our pupils with a physical disability took to the track. Henry was normally in a wheelchair, but he wasn't having that on sports day. At the off, he raced four of his classmates down the sprint track with such glee on his face that no one was watching who won; the whole year group cheered him on to the finish line, and there wasn't a dry eye from the adults on the field. It was a beautiful moment that reminded me of memories from Olympics gone by. All of that was dashed though when the words 'teacher race' were mentioned…

Even for those of us who weren't sporty in school (me!) and aren't sporty as an adult (also me!), there is something brilliant about school sports days. I've seen them across different schools, and no matter the size, setting or demographic, every single school has got stuck in to putting on the best day it could for its pupils.

Why is sports day so important? It might be a fun day out of class in the summer term to keep spirits high, but it's also a super opportunity to showcase sporting talent and give those who might not be academic a platform to shine. Throughout this book I have mentioned the 'whole child' and how important it is that we develop all aspects of our pupils. As teachers, we want them to get the best test scores and make progress, but we similarly want them to realise, develop, practise and display their talents. I have met and worked with many children who are incredibly gifted within sporting disciplines and, as their teacher, I want to champion those talents as much as I would their aptitude for maths, reading and writing.

There have been discussions in the press and social media groups where people have advocated for 'non-competitive' sports days focusing solely on celebrating and challenging ourselves as individuals. I hear what they're saying, but for me, sports days are the perfect place to model the positive values and attitudes that we try to nurture in schools. It's truly heart-warming to see everyone balancing their competitiveness with respect, kindness and resilience. I find it moving when I hear children chanting for their teammates, or even their opponents, willing them on to do well. Life is a competition, and it's best to prepare pupils for the world they are growing up into; I wouldn't want any of my past pupils not aiming high in their future because they are scared to compete for their goals.

When sports day is over and you're reflecting on the buzz you've experienced, remember that it can provide excellent evidence for the Teachers' Standards too.

Standard		Evidence
1	High expectations	This is a brilliant opportunity to demonstrate that you have high expectations of pupils outside the classroom and that it isn't just about academia. Challenging children's attitudes, values and behaviour is just as important!

Standard		Evidence
7	Managing behaviour	Sports day can be chaotic (I'm just warning you). Getting involved in managing the behaviour of a pupil, group, class or whole school could be on the cards, so any reflection on what you or others do to help with this could be secure evidence.
8	Professional behaviours	Getting involved and being a role model (not necessary of the sport, but of the values) contributes massively towards events like sports day. Your participation, and any evidence of it, is a good example of you reaching Teachers' Standard 8.

Top tips and tricks

1. Know your place – not a threat, but a key piece of advice! Some schools' sports days are well-oiled machines with practised plans that run like clockwork. Listen to what is expected of you and do what you can with energy and humour. There's nothing to stop you offering your ideas if you think they'd help.

2. Get stuck in. Even if you aren't sporty, like I wasn't when I started teaching, the day is still a chance to get involved (and get a tan). Interact with the children and make the most of the experience.

3. Stay sun safe. It isn't every day that you get paid to enjoy some sunshine (and maybe even start the

summer bronzing), but you don't want to suffer from sunburn for the rest of the week. Have a hat to hand and slap on the SPF before heading out.

4. Give encouragement to those who need it. For me as a pupil, sports days were a nightmare. I only enjoyed the ones where I felt part of a team because of the support from my peers and my teachers. If you see someone struggling, be there for them.

5. Be competitive. It's all right to have healthy competition, and most adults in a school will have their allegiances (even if they announce that they aren't competitive at all). Now, on to the teacher race – elbows out!

34 The little things

Some days in the classroom are far from easy, and this was one of those days. I'd had a meeting before school that overran; the children had been waiting for me in the rain, so they came in soaked; maths had been an uphill struggle and still none of them could tell the time by the end; and my English lesson resulted in a substantial pile of marking with my name on it. Two minutes before lunchtime, the wet break bell ran, just as I put my seventh pupil on the warning cloud. The incessant rain matched the unforgiving nature of the classroom throughout the morning. My lunch consisted of an instant soup and two paracetamols before I found a quiet corner to take a deep breath. Despite my forced optimism, the afternoon hadn't been much better, and by the time 3.15 pm flashed up on my watch – and I promptly pushed the class out of the door – I couldn't wait to get home and draw a line under my day. But when I was mid-sigh, the all-too-familiar email notification sound rang out from my cupboard.

'Great!'

Luckily, the line in the staff handbook telling us not to be sarcastic didn't apply once the class had gone home.

After going to the staffroom to make a cup of tea and mentally preparing myself for the 90 books I had to mark, I braced myself to read the message.

'I just wanted to email you to say that my daughter has come home today…'

'Here we go,' I thought. Dread kicked in as I slurped a mouthful from my mug.

> '… my daughter has come home today and proudly shown us that she can now tell the time on our kitchen clock. We've been trying for years to teach her, but it seems three days of maths with you have done the trick. She's grinning from ear to ear, and we couldn't be prouder. We're taking her out this evening to get a new watch that she wants to show you tomorrow. We wanted to say how grateful we are for all you've done for her and how fantastic you have been as her teacher. The class are lucky to have you. Enjoy your evening, and many thanks.'

I sat back from the screen and realised I had started crying, despite the huge smile across my face. It's funny how tension, dread and that grey-cloud feeling can just melt away when someone takes the time to show you how appreciated you are and tells you that you are good enough. It was then that I decided to save emails like this to help me on those tough days. I printed it out, found a cardboard folder and the Smile File was born.

The next morning, I came into work on a high and took great pride in hearing that it was 8.48 am, according to the pink watch that now adorned the wrist of my newest time-teller.

Before going further, I want to remind you of my promise of honesty. This chapter reflects on the importance of mental health and broaches the possibility of a 'wobble' in your early years. I'd be lying if I said it didn't happen to most of us, but I'd also be lying if I said it makes us any less worthy of being a teacher.

Newsflash: teaching is not the easy job that many think it is. There are days when you feel overworked and overwhelmed, undervalued and underappreciated. However, many other days leave you with moments that make you feel like you could teach forever and that you have won the game that is life. We often dwell on the negatives and forget to focus on the positives; I get told that it's a teacher thing. My opinion? The popular saying tells us that 'the little things matter', and they all add up; it's important to focus on the highs and capitalise on those happy 'little things', so that we can get something wonderful from our careers.

An increasingly essential element of teaching is looking after your mental health. A survey by the teachers' union NASUWT in 2022 found that 90 per cent of teachers had experienced an increase in work-related stress during the previous 12 months. In 2023, the DfE published their annual school workforce statistics, which told us only 68.7 per cent of newly qualified teachers stayed in the profession past the five-year mark, with 12.8% leaving within the first year. These stats feel scary, but my intention isn't to frighten anyone away; instead, I want to shout from the school rooftops that if you ever find yourself in this situation there are ways of discovering your passion for teaching again, because you deserve to see that you are a wonderful teacher. In my experience, keeping yourself motivated and challenged ensures that you'll get the most from the job. Having a folder of appreciative emails, children's work, praise from your colleagues and things that remind you why you are a teacher is a powerful way of reflecting on what you have achieved so far and maintaining your drive and determination. On the days when I sit down and wonder whether teaching is still for me, I reach for my file and look back at the victories and the moments when I made a difference. Those 'little things' are why I do what I do, and it always makes me to realise what I have achieved.

Talking to other people and sharing the small wins with your colleagues is also a brilliant way of finding the value in and appreciation for what you do. Some of my favourite moments have been those spent with my work friends after tackling something tough and challenging. I'll never forget sitting down to breakfast with my year team on the final day of a residential trip in February 2020. We celebrated the imminent end of the trip, but also that we had managed to give a group of 120 children the opportunity to be children and enjoy special life experiences with their friends (which in hindsight was incredibly poignant considering the national lockdowns that came four weeks later). Other memories that stick in my mind for those tough days include getting told by a mentor and year leader that 'the sun always shines in James's class, no matter the weather outside of it' and the moment when we found out that I'd managed to get three focus children to the expected standard in all of their Year 6 SATs after signs suggested that was never going to happen.

Talking about the negatives is equally important when you're not feeling your best. Your ECT mentor is always there when you need to talk, and you will have colleagues who can offer a shoulder to cry on and a listening ear when you need them to. I found it quite touching when I first got to be on the other side of the conversation and was there to console new teachers and offer them the same reassurance that had been given to me. Remember, no matter how tough the job gets, there is never a time when there are no positives to find. Sometimes it just takes someone else to help you identify them.

Many of us teachers live for those small moments that prove we are doing well and making an impact on the children we teach. Celebrate them, collect them and look back at them regularly so that you can remind yourself how brilliant you are and how lucky we are to have you with us on the front line.

In terms of the Teachers' Standards, all physical evidence (such as positive parent emails, observation feedback and comments from children) could be used to demonstrate that you are hitting standards.

Top tips and tricks

1. Create your own smile file – a place to put emails, feedback, work and mementos from the good days and the successes that you have worked hard to earn.
2. Take time to acknowledge the little wins and positives. It is easy to overlook these and only focus on areas to improve, but remember that you've earned the praise and that it proves your capabilities.

The little things

3. Use positive feedback to shape your personal development. When you receive tough feedback or targets, reflect on the positives that you have also achieved and think about how you can build on those further.

4. Be open and honest with your ECT mentor. Remember that your mentor is there to help you through the highs and lows. Celebrate your achievements and discuss the tough moments so that they can guide and support you.

5. Copy or reference positive feedback in your reflections and evidence. A photocopy of a form or a printout of an email can be strong evidence for some standards (especially Teachers' Standard 8).

35 Countdowns to everything

Lesson by lesson. Day by day. Week by week. Half term by half term. I'd realised how much the job saw me counting down to the next thing on my agenda or in the diary. I wondered if it was because of the sense of the job never being finished or the constant need for the next break! Assessment weeks, pupil progress meetings, assemblies, CPD sessions, observations, mentor meetings, deadlines, half terms, ends of terms… the list of things was so vast that I felt like a human countdown app. Now, though, the countdowns were nearly over.

When I sat down to have lunch in the staffroom, the conversation was firmly fixed on Friday – the last day of the year. People were discussing their plans for the holidays: seeing family, going away, DIY, 'me time', planning! Whatever our ideas were, there was one thing that we all agreed on: the year had gone quickly. In theory, school years are only 11 months long (the remaining month is always made up of the summer holiday) but, looking back now, it felt like yesterday that I'd been doing the register on that fateful first day. I smiled at the memory and the realisation that so much had happened since.

I decided to pick the brains of my more experienced colleagues further, because I wondered if, like in life, the years passed more quickly as you spent more time in schools. Apparently, that was very much the case.

'The first decade feels quite slow, the second speeds up quite considerably and any year over 21 goes by in a blink.'

Truth be told, I felt that was quite sad. Don't get me wrong, I was more than ready for the summer holidays, and I was immensely proud of what I had managed to achieve in my first year of teaching. But Friday would be the end of an era. I wouldn't get to go back to being the newbie again or re-experience the start of my career. I'd lose some of my PPA time too (which was going to hurt). I'd been counting down to that week for ages, and now it had come, I didn't know if I was ready for it.

Since the end of my first year, this inner turmoil of both wanting to and not wanting to count down to everything has really played on my mind. There are days that I'd happily see flash past me, and I often end up flicking through my diary to work out how many days I have until the next long weekend or half-term break. But in a job where we say we never have enough time, is some of the problem that we wish our time away?

When it comes to the workload, I could always do with more time. As I sit at my desk on a Friday afternoon, I look at my 'to do' list and jot down unfinished tasks on the following week's page in my notebook. Looking at what those jobs are, I usually realise that if I hadn't been so keen to cross the day off the calendar so quickly, I might have been able to stay an additional ten minutes and get an extra task done. I don't want to spend every moment in the school building, and I need to make sure I have that work–life balance, but maybe I could be more efficient with the hours and minutes I have.

Then comes the feeling that I didn't get to value the time I had because I was too busy counting it away. Remember when you were a child, looking out of the car window? If the car was going fast, you could blink and miss something outside as you zoomed past it. If it was going slower, you could see what was out there a lot more clearly, and you could appreciate it more. Time moves at its own pace (I haven't managed to get the time machine up and running yet), but we can influence the way we perceive it. Over the years, I've come to realise that while I can carry on counting down to the next milestone, deadline or big event, I need to look back as much as forward and consider what's happened. I take more time now to value each day when it's over and think about what I've achieved and learned. Not only does that help slow down my perception of time, but it means I learn from it, making it more impactful. It stops me thinking that I've just blinked and missed it. I remember being in the staffroom on that final week and feeling that overwhelming sense of 'where has the year gone?'. Time had never moved so quickly for me as a 22-year-old. Now though, each year passes more rapidly than the last, and the years tally up as quickly as the months did at the beginning. Each September brings a new class that I work with, teach, mould, train and guide through our three terms together, and then they wave goodbye as I stay put and start the cycle again. It can feel relentless as well as rewarding, but I always come away from it thinking that I wish I'd had more time.

I suppose the reason I wanted to share this is because I want to prepare you for the feeling of the end of the school year and encourage you to stop rushing towards it while you still can. If it's been a good year, you'll finish with a mix of euphoria and loss. If it hasn't, relief might be the more overwhelming emotion. The end of the year will always happen eventually, but make sure you don't get sucked into losing track of time. Enjoy the moments before they become memories.

Top tips and tricks

1. Take every day as it comes. Once a day is done, you won't experience it, or another day quite like it, again. Enjoy the good days, but don't wish away the bad ones; value them for what they are.

2. Try to avoid countdowns. This is easier said than done, especially with some of your colleagues. I stopped writing countdowns in my diary or on my whiteboard because it just made everything a bit depressing.

3. Focus on fun milestones instead. If you and your class want something to focus on and count down to, go for something like a trip or experience. It's much more satisfying than the next break!

4. Celebrate what's already happened as well as looking forward. Many teachers focus on what is coming up and hardly ever look back on what has been. As a new teacher, remember the things you have achieved to balance your excitement for the next thing on the calendar.

5. Mix things up. If you find yourself stuck counting down through days of mundanity, try something new to revitalise yourself and your class. Could you change some lessons around? Is there a trip or experience you could add to some upcoming learning? Could you change your setting for a lesson and do some maths outside, for example?

36 The final day of the year

Dear Future Me, it's 11.00 am on your first day as a teacher, and your class are writing their letters to their future selves. Things are going well so far, so I thought I'd write a note for you to open with them on the last day.

What a year it must have been! How does it feel sitting there on the other side? You've completed it… or at least I hope you have. Truth be told, I'm nervous about what's to come, so hopefully it hasn't been too chaotic. Did you manage to escape Ofsted? Were the class good for you? How was the residential?

Most importantly, how were the observations and assessments? Did we pass?!

Whatever happened, I want you to know I'm proud of you for everything you've achieved, more so than anyone else. I know how scary this journey has been, and now, as long as you are still standing at the end of it, you've managed to prove yourself as a teacher. I hope the year has been as rewarding as we hoped and that we will be doing it again in September!

Right, back to reality. Break starts in five minutes! Just 189 days to go…

From Past You

If you are reading this chapter on the final day of your first year, I want to start by saying congratulations. You made it! You have done something incredible this year and made your mark on the lives of some lucky children, who will hopefully one day share what you've taught them and put it to good use. I hope it has been everything you wanted it to be and more. Plus, as you read earlier on, one in eight new teachers don't make it past this day, so if you're coming back for Round Two next year, even more respect to you. We appreciate you and want you back with us!

The last day of my first year was a real mix of emotions, and it started an annual tradition of me crying as I said goodbye to each and every class that moved on. I can't describe the feeling in one word, but it was like a combination of surreality, sadness, relief, excitement and exhaustion rolled into one. I'd done it. Completed it. Tick! But I was sad to have got to the end of the chapter. I had put my all into these children, and I wasn't really ready to say goodbye.

On that final Friday, we listened to Year 6 sobbing their way through a rendition of 'Goodbye My Friend', signed the shirts of any pupil (or staff member) leaving that summer and opened up our time capsule from the first day. It was a lovely moment when the pupils read back their letters from their past selves and realised how much they had grown over that time. I read mine too, and laughed about the Ofsted question. No, I hadn't managed to miss the inspection, but I was safe for at least another three years. The day was full of opportunities to look back, and I believe it's important that we do. As a new teacher on your first last day of school, you have made it through one of the toughest years of your teaching career. While things will be challenging in the future, they are rarely as intense as they have been for you over the last 12 months.

The other big event of that last day for me was handing out the children's end-of-year reports. Behind the scenes, I'd spent three months writing over 60,000 words, all while applying my best tactical teacher vocabulary to balance reality with the avoidance of any last-minute complaints. It had been a challenge, but I felt incredibly proud of managing to get the project completed and was pleased to be sending my pupils home with their big brown envelopes, knowing that they'd be reasons for everyone to smile when they read them at home.

At the end of the day the bell rang, and as the children said their last goodbyes to me and the classroom, the year was over. What hit me was a sense of numbness and not knowing how to feel. It felt like I was starting to mourn the finished year already. They say your first class is always your favourite – would I ever get a class as good as this lot? The tears returned, but I didn't know which emotion was causing them. It didn't help that I'd opened the card my class had made me and unwrapped the gift from the class parents. While they could be hard work at times, I would miss the parents too!

Minutes after the last child left, staff were piling out the doors, bags and car keys in hand. No one waits around on the last day, but I was grateful to get lots of people popping in to congratulate me for making it through the year. It all just felt very surreal, and I wondered if it would sink in soon or not until I woke up on Monday without an alarm. All I knew was that my focus right then was getting out of the building. I'd long had the plan of driving out of the school gates with the windows and sunroof open and 'School's Out' playing loud from the stereo. So, at 2.00 pm, I locked the classroom door, put on my shades and got into the car. I drove past the park outside the school and was met with cheers from my class as they spotted my car and waved me off for my first summer holidays as a teacher. I'd earned it. I'd done it.

End-of-year checklist

The best advice I can give you for the last day is a list of things to get done before you walk off into the sunset for the summer.

- Check the expectations for books, trays, locker labels, labels, etc. Some schools will be environmentally friendly or save time by passing certain things up with the children.
- Sort out any piles of paperwork around the classroom, especially if they are pieces of old work. This is your last chance to give them out before they end up being filed under 'B' for 'bin'.
- Ask your children to bring in an extra bag for the final day, so that you can send them home with

more stuff than normal. There's nothing worse than the parent coming back to ask if you can hold on to their work until September because they can't carry it home that day.

- Ensure that reports are sent home if they haven't been already. There is an expectation that they are sent home a week before the final day, but this isn't always the case.

- Make sure your class empty everything! There is nothing worse than coming back in September to a fruit-fly infestation caused by a left-behind banana or having to extract a festering PE bag that was missed in the end-of-year sweep.

- Moving classrooms? Get as much done as possible before the summer holidays, especially when you have lots of hands to help. I once got my whole class to each take a bag or box to my new room on the last day to help save my back.

- Enjoy the moments with your class – they will forever be your first set of pupils and, regardless of whether you've loved or loathed them, they will always be memorable. Take the time you deserve to appreciate what you've done for them.

- Clear your desk of any unnecessary clutter and paper before you go, so that you can come back to a clean start in September. Watch out for any washing-up, too – I've seen some people's final July coffees looking horrific come September.

- Is a child unexpectedly absent on the last day? Either ask their parents to come in to collect their things or send them up in a bag to their new teacher to be picked up in September.

- Take an electronic copy of your planning for the following year so that you can begin working on it during the summer holidays. Don't rely on remote access if your school has this, as it can be unreliable.

- Meet with your new year team or colleagues to discuss what you need to do over the summer to prepare for the new year.

- Double-check that your induction and ECT paperwork is completed and sent off before the summer break so you don't have it hanging over your head as you start your second year.

- Switch off the computer, the lights and any other electronics… and head out that door!

37 Young versus old

Teaching is a strange profession when it comes to age. As a newly qualified teacher on the front line, I went from feeling very young to very old very quickly!

I am a 'summer-born', so all through my life I have been one of the youngest in my year groups and in most friendship circles. It's been a part of life as I've grown up, and I've become accustomed to being the young one wherever I go. When I started my first teaching role, I stood in front of my first class at the age of 22 years and 4 days old; if I hadn't taken a year out to try and earn some money to afford university, I would have theoretically been one of the youngest teachers in the country ever! But, as soon as I finished my first few days in the new role, I realised that age doesn't matter in schools; it soon becomes the case that the children are all in one age bracket and the staff are all in another.

The other new teacher who started at the same time as me was older – she had a husband, two children, a big house and a dog. We were in very different stages of life, but here we were, taking the same step on the same journey. It was humbling to be shoulder to shoulder with someone who had more life experience but to whom I was an equal. It soon made me realise that being on 'Team Teacher' means you have common ground and age becomes insignificant.

As a teacher, I love the fact that I get to work with people of all backgrounds, races, religions and ages. I've had colleagues who have come into schools and overtaken me as the youngest, others who have celebrated milestone birthdays and even others who have retired. Some of these colleagues, who often become work friends and even good friends, have been further from my age than my pupils are. Teaching probably sees this happening more than many other jobs and industries. I remember laughing with three colleagues during my first year while at the pub on a Friday after work because it would be unlikely to see two twenty-somethings out drinking with two people in their fifties otherwise. It only got worse when the older two realised they could be the mothers of us younger ones. The truth was we'd been working together for months and didn't even realise the gap between us all; we just knew we were an effective team with four different perspectives to bring to the table, and it worked like a charm.

While writing this book and working as a supply teacher across many different schools, I've been able to meet some brilliant practitioners and some inspiring new teachers, who I know for a fact will bring much to the industry. Each one of them has their own experiences and background, providing their own perspective and energy to their classroom and school. Again, that's something brilliant about our profession: it doesn't matter how old you are, you bring yourself to your class, and that's what counts.

The moral of the story is: if you are a 'mature' student joining the profession later in life, don't worry, because I can guarantee that being in the classroom will make you feel young and no one will even notice. And if you're young, like I was, you soon won't feel it, especially when you realise what year your pupils were born!

38 Outside perceptions

Over the months that I have spent writing this book, the teaching and education industry have been under the usual scrutiny and watchful eye of the public and the press.

Social media, as mentioned earlier in this book, can be tough to tackle when you become a teacher. Not only is it a place where your pupils and their parents might catch a glimpse into your personal life (all of which can be misinterpreted, so be mindful) but it's a platform on which anyone is entitled to air their opinions and throw shade at those of us on the front line. I try hard to bite my virtual tongue when I'm reading posts about how ungrateful teachers are when we get so much time off, how lazy we are for doing six-hour days and how those who can't do anything well enough end up as teachers. We know ourselves that those thoughts and perspectives are total rubbish, and while I accept free speech, I also think it's important that we have a world where people can be challenged on potential misinformation.

Celebrities and public figures are often encouraged to stay away from hearsay, and they have support to get them through bad press and PR. As someone who has worked in the media industry, I've had my fair share of unwanted messages and opinions, and I know how tough it can be to keep a smile on your face. Unfortunately, in teaching we don't always get the support with this we deserve, and on several occasions I've seen colleagues and friends feeling really upset by news articles, posts and campaigns that insult and belittle us and what we do.

My advice for any teacher, new or not, is: think carefully about how you use social media. Along with following the normal warnings about keeping profiles private and considering what you make public, think too about how you use platforms like Twitter, Instagram and TikTok as a spectator. These are brilliant for classroom inspiration, display ideas and lesson suggestions, but they can also be home to trolls and generally unkind people with thoughts that we could really do without.

If you are a bit of a Twitter trawler or spend time 'doomscrolling', just be aware. If you see posts that are complaining about teachers or making light of the unfortunate issues in our industry, switch off and leave them be. My recommendation is always to walk away and not enter the arena. I've seen examples of teachers trying to do battle, airing their opinions and losing spectacularly, sometimes ending up with a disciplinary for what they've posted online in the public domain.

Rest assured though, the important people know how much you do and how hard you work. Your pupils value you, as do their parents and your colleagues. Our job isn't easy, but as long as we all support each other, we can do it!

39 Desk-chair days

I'll fully admit that there have been times in my teaching career when I've thought about packing it all in to go and work in an office somewhere. Think about it: no work to take home, switching off at 5.00 pm and walking out with a clear mind, your own space to work, fewer people to manage, the ability to go to the toilet when you need to, an entire break time to yourself… sounds like bliss, right?

For many of us, being a teacher is about the actual teaching and working with the brilliant young minds of children. It's a unique profession, and it won't suit everybody, which is why I firmly believe that those of us in classrooms across the world are all born to teach. Some say it's because we possess a natural 'something' that makes us want to do what we do; I just deduce that we are suited to the ways of the job – being constantly up and about, speaking in front of others, thinking on our feet, managing behaviour (playing 'educational whack-a-mole', as I call it), monitoring data, being a Jack of all trades and dealing with the all-too-frequent curveballs that are hurled at us. If you can manage all of that while maintaining a smile for most of the day, you were born to teach! I can see why no one has ever asked me to write the job description for a teacher…

Every now and then, we might get lucky and win the prize of a 'desk-chair day' – my name for a day out of class when I can squirrel myself away with a cup of tea and some biscuits and power through the endless list of forms, admin work and planning that always needs to be done – the side of teaching that many people don't realise we juggle with the actual classroom part of the job. I consider these days a welcome break from the frenzy at the whiteboard and see them as a glimpse into what life could have been like if I weren't a teacher. I don't know where or what I'd be if I hadn't chosen this career path, but a desk job has always sounded like a solid option. I know it isn't the same, but my occasional opportunities to work with my headphones on, powering through a list of jobs, managing my own time without too many disruptions and eating lunch when I want to are, quite frankly, a luxury. Any time I require a trip back to the classroom, it's nice to see the children, because I miss them (although I wouldn't admit it out loud), but it's equally nice to get back out of there and return to the serenity of my temporary workspace. It all just feels so refreshing and free… that is, until the afternoon.

Again, if you're a teacher, you need to have a passion for the job, and you'll usually find there's something that pulls you back to where you're 'meant to be'. By 2.00 pm, my attention will have wandered off, and I'll be bored; I'll sneak into the staffroom to catch up with the daily gossip, and at any opportunity, I will pop into the classroom again, just to make sure that everything's all right. Has Johnny managed to stay off the red traffic light? Did Samira at least try the extension activity, like she knows she should? Are they all behaving or showing me up? Just before the home bell rings, without fail, I'm back in there to say goodbye to the children, make sure the room is tidy and answer any end-of-the-day questions. It's funny how the excitement of escaping the classroom seems to disappear as you slowly realise you miss it. I just can't stay away.

By the end of my desk-chair days, as much as I love them, I know that I'm looking forward to teaching again the next day. That pull is one of the strangest things about our profession, especially as the longer you stay in teaching and the higher you move up the ladder, the less time you spend with the children. I always welcome a bit of change to my routine and a bit of a breather to help me catch up with my work, but I can never be out of the classroom for long. It reminds me that I am in the right place and doing the right thing. Always a positive realisation to have!

40 Funny moments

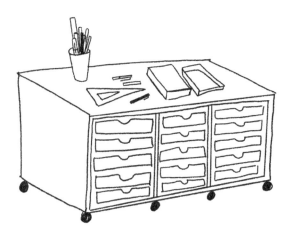

The French writer Nicolas Chamfort said that 'a day without laughter is a day wasted'. He was right.

Working in schools, there is no shortage of times when a belly laugh, a snicker or a snort is the only way that you and your brain can react. I've cried laughing at candid moments in class when something unexpectedly hilarious has happened, and I've laughed crying during emotional end-of-year goodbyes. I've giggled in meetings, chuckled at the staffroom table and faked coughing fits to hide my laughter in assemblies (so unprofessional). I've laughed at myself and laughed with others (sometimes at them too). I've laughed when someone has tried to brighten my day and laughed to brighten the days of others. Laughter is a powerful tool to make life better, and my ambition is to work in a classroom and a school full of it. My advice for new teachers is to aim for the same.

Don't listen to the classic advice of not smiling until Christmas; if you want to add some humour, do so. Knowing your children well – which Teachers' Standard 1 and Teachers' Standard 5 both encourage – enables you to appeal to their funny bones and establish that oh-so-important rapport. Now, you don't need or want to be your pupils' friend (that can make your job a lot harder), but making a little quip about their football team or sharing a funny story about their favourite animal can let your children know you value them. I wouldn't call it all-out banter, but some children love a bit of wit and relish the chance to joke with a person who they trust and respect. I often think I'm enabling them to practise good social skills (including knowing when to stop!).

Some of my most treasured moments in schools are those when I can get a class to laugh along with me and make them feel like they can be part of the joke. It means a lot to children. I often hear at parents' evenings, or from parents on the playground at the end of the day, what children have shared with their families over the dinner table. One such mealtime memory came from a time when I was perched on a unit of the pupils' plastic trays (you know the ones). While teaching, I'd managed to manoeuvre my hands into one of the top trays, and as I went to stand up I realised that I was stuck. Zane had put his tray in back to front, and I'd unluckily found the one tray that had been jammed in. I tried styling it out and kept teaching from the front. I got the children set on their task and then subtly attempted to remove my hand, my wrist getting number and redder with every minute that passed. Much to the amusement of my class, I gave up after five minutes and wheeled the unit down the corridor, hand still attached, to get some help from the office. To say it was embarrassing is an understatement, but I laughed it off, and it was hilarious seeing the children giggle as they recognised that teachers make mistakes too. It became a running joke for the rest of my first year, cropping up at parents' evenings and in our 'funny memories' English task. In fact, it even appeared two years on as Zane's memory in the Year 6 leavers' assembly. It still makes me laugh now.

Mishaps in children's work are a treat to encounter when you're knee deep in marking, and they're another regular source of laughter on which you can rely. Whether it's ancient Egyptians 'rapping up mummies' in bandages (presumably to a sick hip-hop beat) or an unfortunate misspelling causing Roald Dahl's Willy Wonka to sound like he should be in an adult film instead of a kids' book, the children never fail to provide me with some comic relief. Just don't ask me what the 'energetic elephant' was doing, according to one of my Year 4 pupils in an alliterative zoo task. Obviously, they'd been learning a bit too much from Willy! I was just glad that I wasn't teaching sex ed for another couple of months.

Your colleagues can be a great source of laughter and fun too, depending on what they are like, of course. I've had planning meetings where I've nearly passed out from laughter and Inset days spent in stitches. I've spat tea across a table at least once too. Guilty! While children can be fountains of hilarity, it's always nice to be able to share some comedy with those in your own age range. Trust me, I've heard some things over a cuppa or a sandwich that would turn the air blue. Some colleagues are outrageous, and it tends to be the quiet ones.

Ultimately, a sense of humour should really be on a teacher's job description, because it helps you remain resilient and make even the dreary days a lot brighter. Having a laugh is a way of de-stressing after a long day, and it frequently makes me thankful for what I do and appreciate the hilarious people I work with. Plus, laughing things off helps you save face when you get your hand stuck in a tray.

Glossary

People always think that being a primary school teacher means you don't need to learn a lot of new information, because 'you did it all at school yourself'. I applaud anyone who is brave enough to say that to me… before I then get on my soapbox and reveal the truth. Not only do we have to keep our subject knowledge refreshed, but teaching brings with it a whole new language – and, wow, we love using initials! For those who haven't yet grasped the difference between CPD, ECT and the DfE, or haven't heard about Zones of Regulation, here's a helpful guide to help you speak 'teacher'.

Department for Education (DfE) This is the government department that is responsible for education and children's services. It has been known by other names in the past, including Department for Education and Skills (DFES) and Department for Children, Schools and Families (DCSF).

Designated Safeguarding Lead (DSL) By law, every school must have a named person who is responsible for leading safeguarding. These are the people with whom you need to share any concerns or disclosures. It is vital that you know who they are when starting in a new school. They might also have deputies, known as DDSLs, in some places.

Differentiation The process of adapting or creating alternative activities that are appropriate for the needs of a child. For example, creating more challenging tasks to stretch more able pupils or providing resources to support those with SEND in completing tasks.

Early Career Framework (ECF) A framework, published by the DfE in 2019, through which new teachers are inducted into the profession and supported through their first two years in the classroom.

Early Career Teacher (ECT) A teacher in their first two years of teaching, as defined by the DfE in the ECF.

Form entry A term used to describe the number of classes in a year group. For example, a three-form-entry school has three classes in each year group. Having a 'bulge' year means that there is at least one additional class over the standard number.

Keeping Children Safe in Education (KCSiE) A statutory guidance document published annually by the DfE, which provides information relating to safeguarding and child protection. It is essential that all teachers read at least the first part of the guidance. Teachers will be asked to sign a document confirming that they have read this and will often undertake safeguarding training to prove this.

Mentor A person who should be designated to support you with your ECT years. They will observe you, meet with you and work with you to complete the ECT assessments and paperwork. They are usually an experienced teacher who has had mentor training.

Newly Qualified Teacher (NQT) The old name for a new teacher, which used to be applied during a teacher's first year of practice.

Planning, Preparation and Assessment (PPA) Time given, as required by law, to allow teachers to plan lessons, prepare for their teaching and assess pupils' work alongside other administrative tasks. For ECTs, this could amount to up to 20 per cent of the teaching week.

Senior Leadership Team (SLT) A team of people who lead the school. Sometimes known as the Senior Management Team (SMT), this group usually consists of the headteacher, deputy headteacher and assistant headteacher, and could include the school business manager (SBM), SENDCo, year leaders and phase leaders.

Special Educational Needs and Disabilities (SEND) A term used to group together any mental or physical need or disability that could alter the way in which a child learns.

Special Educational Needs and Disabilities Coordinator (SENDCo) The person or people responsible for overseeing a school's SEND provision. They are sometimes known as the SENCo or inclusion manager.

Teachers' Standards Produced by the DfE, the eight Teachers' Standards (alongside the 'Part Two' section) are used to support, train and appraise teachers in the UK.

Teaching assistant (TA) Known by many titles nowadays, including learning support assistant (LSA) and classroom assistant (CA), this is the role of the adults working with you in the classroom to help specific pupils or your wider class to get the most from their learning. A valuable resource when utilised well.

Zones of Regulation Created by Leah Kuypers, the Zones of Regulation is a framework and curriculum tool that aims to support children in understanding, identifying and regulating their emotions.

References

Brown, S. (2021) 'Assemblies: why they matter and how to improve them. *TES*, 19th August. Available at: https://www.tes.com/magazine/archived/assemblies-why-they-matter-and-how-improve-them (Accessed:09.06.2023)

Department for Education (2016) *Standard for teachers' development*. Available at: https://assets.publishing.service.gov.uk/government/uploads/system/uploads/attachment_data/file/537031/160712_-_PD_Expert_Group_Guidance.pdf (Accessed: 09.06.2023)

Department for Education (2020) *Governance handbook*. Available at: https://assets.publishing.service.gov.uk/government/uploads/system/uploads/attachment_data/file/925104/Governance_Handbook_FINAL.pdf (Accessed: 09.06.2023)

Department for Education (2021) *Teachers' Standards*. Available at: https://assets.publishing.service.gov.uk/government/uploads/system/uploads/attachment_data/file/1040274/Teachers__Standards_Dec_2021.pdf (Accessed: 09.06.2023)

Department for Education (2023) *Induction for early career teachers (England)*. Available at: https://www.gov.uk/government/publications/induction-for-early-career-teachers-england (Accessed: 09.06.2023)

Department for Education (2023) *School workforce in England*. Available at: https://explore-education-statistics.service.gov.uk/find-statistics/school-workforce-in-england. (Accessed: 09.06.2023)

Department for Education and Skills (2006) *Learning Outside The Classroom Manifesto*. Available at: https://oeapng.info/

downloads/download-info/2-2a-lotc-manifesto-publication/ (Accessed: 09.06.2023)

Education Policy Institute, Wellcome Trust (2021) *The effects of high-quality professional development on teachers and students.* Available at: https://epi.org.uk/wp-content/uplo ads/2021/04/EPI-CPD-entitlement-cost-benefit-analysis.2021. pdf (Accessed: 09.06.2023)

Hawkes, N. (2000) *Being a School of Excellence: The Role of the School Assembly.* Available at: https://livingvalues.net/reference/ being-a-school-of-excellence-the-role-of-the-school-assembly (Accessed: 09.06.2023)

NASUWT (2022) *Teacher Wellbeing Survey – 2022.* Available at: https://www.nasuwt.org.uk/static/1ac040a7-96a5-481a- a052ddd850abc476/Teacher-Wellbeing-Survey-Report-2022. pdf (Accessed: 09.06.2023)

National Governance Association (2023) *Eight elements of effective governance.* Available at: https://www.nga.org.uk/Knowledge- Centre/Good-governance/Effective-governance/Eight-Eleme nts-of-Effective-Governance.aspx (Accessed: 09.06.2023)

NHS (2023) *How to fall asleep faster and sleep better.* Available at: https://www.nhs.uk/every-mind-matters/mental- wellbeing-tips/how-to-fall-asleep-faster-and-sleep-better/ (Accessed: 09.06.2023)

NI Direct (2023) *How play helps children's development.* Available at: https://www.nidirect.gov.uk/articles/how-play-helps-childr ens-development#:~:text=Play%20improves%20the%20cognit ive%2C%20physical,confidence (Accessed: 09.06.2023)

Office for Standards in Education (2008) *Learning outside the classroom – How far should you go?* Available at: https://dera.ioe. ac.uk/id/eprint/9253/1/Learning%20outside%20the%20classr oom.pdf (Accessed: 09.06.2023)

Office for Standards in Education (2011) *Schools and parents.* Available at: https://assets.publishing.service.gov.uk/governm ent/uploads/system/uploads/attachment_data/file/413696/ Schools_and_parents.pdf (Accessed at 09.06.2023)

Office for Standards in Education (2022) *School Inspection Handbook.* Available at: https://www.gov.uk/government/publications/ school-inspection-handbook-eif/school-inspection-handb ook#clarification-for-schools (Accessed: 09.06.2023)

Office for Standards in Education (2023) *About us.* Available at: https://www.gov.uk/government/organisations/ofsted/about (Accessed: 09.06.2023)

Paul Hamlyn Foundation (2015) *Learning Away final evaluation: full report.* Available at: https://www.phf.org.uk/publications/learn ing-away-final-evaluation-full-report/ (Accessed: 09.06.2023)

Paul Hamlyn Foundation (2015) *Learning Away final evaluation: full report.* Available at: https://www.phf.org.uk/publications/learn ing-away-final-evaluation-full-report/ (Accessed: 09.06.2023)

Paul Hamlyn Foundation (2015) *Learning Away.* Available at: https://www.phf.org.uk/programmes/learning-away-2/ (Accessed: 09.06.2023)

Social Mobility Commission (2019) *An unequal playing field: extra-curricular activities, soft skills and social mobility.* Available at: https://www.gov.uk/government/publicati ons/extra-curricular-activities-soft-skills-and-social-mobility/ an-unequal-playing-field-extra-curricular-activities-soft-ski lls-and-social-mobility (Accessed: 09.06.2023)

The Education Endowment Foundation (2021) *Improving Social and Emotional Learning in Primary Schools.* Available at: https://educa tionendowmentfoundation.org.uk/education-evidence/guida nce-reports/primary-sel (Accessed: 09.06.2023)

The Education Endowment Foundation (2021) *Parental engagement.* Available at: https://educationendowmentfoundation.org.uk/

education-evidence/teaching-learning-toolkit/parental-eng agement (Accessed: 09.06.2023)

The Education Endowment Foundation (2021) *Parental engagement*. Available at: https://educationendowmentfoundation.org.uk/ education-evidence/teaching-learning-toolkit/physical-activity (Accessed: 09.06.2023)

The Education Endowment Foundation (2021) *Teacher Feedback To Improve Pupil Learning – Guidance Report*. Available at: https://education endowmentfoundation.org.uk/ education-evidence/guidance-reports/feedback?gclid=Cj wKCAjwvdajBhBEEiwAeMh1UwpB8hv0UKxXNYu8Uxl4FLw MtVbt4LAD8PZDH6HjCE7tAeseWZTWahoCIE4QAvD_BwE (Accessed: 09.06.2023)

Wiliam, D. (2019) 'Dylan Wiliam: Teaching not a research-based profession', *TES*, 30th May 2019. Available at: https://www. tes.com/magazine/archive/dylan-wiliam-teaching-not-resea rch-based-profession (Accessed: 09.06.2023)

Willis, J. (2014) 'Teacher's guide to sleep – and why it matters', *The Guardian*, November 11th. Available at: https://www.theg uardian.com/teacher-network/teacher-blog/2014/nov/11/ good-night-teacher-guide-sleep (Accessed: 09.06.2023)

Winter, B. et al. (2007) 'High impact running improves learning', *Neurobiology of Learning and Memory*, 87(4), pp. 597-609.

Index of Teachers' Standards

The Teachers' Standards 'define the minimum level of practice expected of trainees and teachers from the point of being awarded qualified teacher status (QTS). The Teachers' Standards are used to assess all trainees working towards QTS, and all those completing their statutory induction period. They are also used to assess the performance of all teachers with QTS…' (DfE, 2021).